Intensive Reading Course on Chinese Culture: Social Life

中国文化精读教程：社会生活

冯薇薇 张超 编著

SinolinguA
华语教学出版社

First Edition 2025

ISBN 978-7-5138-2563-4

Published by Sinolingua Co., Ltd
24 Baiwanzhuang Street, Beijing 100037, China
Tel: (86)10-68320585, 68997826
Fax: (86)10-68997826, 68326333
http://www.sinolingua.com.cn
E-mail: hyjx@sinolingua.com.cn
Facebook: www.facebook.com/sinolingua
Printed by Beijing Hucais Culture Communication Co., Ltd

Printed in the People's Republic of China

前　言

《中国文化精读教程》是参照《国际中文教育中文水平等级标准》和《国际中文教育用中国文化和国情教学参考框架》的指导和要求开发而成的系列教程。本系列教程语言难度控制在《国际中文教育中文水平等级标准》中级的水平，文化理解的分级目标控制在《参考框架》中级阶段，可应用于海外各个国家中学到大学阶段，亦可与国际中文教育精读课程（中级）相结合。

本系列教程共三册，每个分册分别对应《参考框架》中级阶段的三大主题——社会生活、传统文化和当代中国，涵盖了15个话题，设置了30篇课文，覆盖80多个文化点，力求完成中级阶段所要求的教学内容和目标，即：了解中国社会生活、传统文化和当代中国国情的基本知识，理解多样性，比较中国文化和本土文化的主要异同。每篇课文的教学内容包括：课文阅读（附英文翻译）、短视频、生词表、语法点、结构分析、练习、文化话题活动。课文的词汇难度控制在4~6级之间，每篇课文包含约20个生词，3~5个成语或惯用语，1~3个语法点。

本系列教程选材兼具趣味性和讨论性。我们精心挑选了一系列文化趣事、社科美文、热点新闻以及爆款视频的文本，确保课程内容丰富多元、动态活泼，力求在体现中华文化深厚底蕴的同时也能反映当下中国社会的热点话题。我们希望这些文章能够引领学生深入探索中国文化的内涵，发现文化差异，拓展视野，激发学生对中华文化和跨文化交际的热情与好奇心。本系列教程中还设计了丰富的文化探究活动和课堂讨论环节，旨在从多个角度、多个层面引导学生探索文化的奥秘，启发学生思考。

我们希望，通过学习本系列教程，学生不仅能够深入了解中华文化，更能够提升跨文化交际敏感度和能力，成为真正具有国际视野的人才。

目录

话题一 饮食

教学内容和目标	文化点
1. 了解中国人的餐桌礼仪和表达的文化含义。 2. 了解中国人饮食方式的变化及影响因素。 3. 了解中国人的饮食和健康观念及其变化。	菜系，公筷，快餐，外卖，美食榜单，中国药膳

课文 1　一百元挑战成都小吃街

课前热身

请仔细观察下面这张图片，用两分钟左右的时间描述一下你在图片上看到了什么，以及你对图片的理解。

课文 1

扫一扫，看视频

一百元挑战成都小吃街

说到成都，除了可爱的大熊猫，不得不说的就是成都的美食。成都有一条“网红”小吃街，每天都热热闹闹，它就是成都建设路小吃街。在这里，花一百元人民币能吃到多少美食？美国人李夏天和他的中国妻子李玲玲来到成都建设路，上演了一场百元大挑战。

李夏天说：“几年前，我们曾经住在这里。最近这里开了很多美食小店，有了天翻地覆的变化，很多当地人和中外游客都会来这里品尝美食小吃。我是吃货，她也是吃货，所以我们一定要来这里打卡。今天我们有一个挑战，看看在这里用一百元能买到多少好吃的！”

“这个多少钱？给我来个小份儿的，对，要辣一点儿！”美国人李夏天说中文很标准，甚至还会说四川方言，令大家十分惊讶。跟着美食的香味，夫妻俩挑战的第一个美食是臭豆腐。李夏天非常喜欢臭豆腐，“臭豆腐，闻着臭吃着香！”但是，他的妻子并不这么认为，即使作为中国人，她也很难接受这个味道。

为了缓解“臭味”，李玲玲买了一杯烧仙草。烧仙草是中国南方特色饮品，把仙草、糯米丸和奶茶混合到一起，冰冰甜甜，夏天喝上一杯，有防暑降温的作用。

他们边走边吃，突然看到了李玲玲最喜欢的火锅鸡爪。鸡爪对很多外国人来说是难以接受的食物，对李夏天来说也是如此。对于鸡爪这种食材，他十分抗拒，只能评价道："我觉得，嗯，还好吧。"他的妻子反驳道："不仅仅是还好吧，简直是太棒了。"

接着他们又发现了另一种美食——鸡翅包糯米饭。鸡翅看起来很诱人，可以说是色香味俱全。李夏天指着招牌，用地道的四川话念道："巴适的板！"（意思是"太棒了"）拿到鸡翅包糯米饭，李夏天尝了一口，"我从来没有吃过这种做法，很有嚼劲，软软的，糯糯的。这个有点儿像是墨西哥菜或西班牙菜。"

在建设路小吃街一路逛下来，这对跨国夫妻的百元挑战也结束了，结果是一百元人民币吃到了好几种美食：臭豆腐、火锅鸡爪、鸡翅包糯米饭、烧仙草、芋圆冰沙、煎饼、脏咖啡流心蛋糕。李夏天说："真是不可思议，我们花一百元竟然吃到了这么多美食。我最喜欢成都的一个原因就是这里的食物又好吃又便宜，只花很少的钱就可以实现'美食自由'。"

A Couple's Challenge: 100 RMB for Snacks in Chengdu

When it comes to Chengdu, in addition to the cute pandas, what we must mention is the food. Chengdu has an "internet-famous" snack street, and is always packed with people. It is a food district on the Jianshe Road. How much food can you get here for 100 RMB yuan?

Lawrence, Chinese name, Li Xiatian, an American, and his Chinese wife, Li Lingling, came to Jianshe Road to meet a challenge: Spend just 100 yuan on snacks.

"We used to live here a few years ago. But in recent years, things have just gotten amazingly insane regarding food quality and quantity. All tourists, local and foreign, like coming here to try the delicious foods," said Lawrence. "I'm a foodie, and my wife's a foodie, too. So, we just have to check it out. Today, we have a challenge: the 100 RMB food challenge. We'll see how much food we can buy with just 100 RMB."

"How much is it? I want a small one. A little more chili!" Despite being an American, Lawrence's Chinese sounded standard, and the Sichuan dialect he blurted out was even more surprising to everyone. Following the scent of food, the couple found their first challenge — stinky tofu. Lawrence thought that stinky tofu smelled very pungent but tasted really good. He felt that was fantastic. However, Lingling, as a Chinese, didn't seem to like the taste at all.

Next, Lingling bought a cup of herbal jelly to lessen the smell of stinky tofu. Herbal jelly is a special traditional drink in south China. It is composed of ingredients like mesona, taro balls and balls of tapioca, then mixed with sweets and cool milk tea, greatly satisfying people's taste buds. Drinking a cup in summer could make people cool down.

As they were eating and walking, they suddenly saw Lingling's favorite — hot-pot chicken feet. Chicken feet as a food are difficult to imagine for Americans. So is Lawrence, he said, "I think it's okay, I would say." Lingling didn't just agree, she said, "It's not just okay. It's wonderful."

They saw someone selling chicken wings stuffed with glutinous rice, which looked very tempting. Pointing to the signboard, Lawrence read in authentic Sichuan dialect, "*Bashideban* (Very good)!"After getting the chicken wings stuffed with glutinous rice, Lawrence tasted a bite, "I've never had things like this before. It's very chewy, soft, and glutinous. It might be like Mexican or Spanish food."

After a round of buying and eating down the Jianshe Road, the couple's challenge ended, resulting in 100 RMB for several foods for each of them: stinky tofu, hot-pot chicken feet, chicken wings stuffed with glutinous rice, herbal jelly, Taro smoothie, pancake, and dirty coffee lava cake. "It is unbelievable that I can buy so many delicious foods for 100 yuan. It's actually my favorite part of my living in Chengdu: The food is delicious and cheap, and you can eat a lot of food with little money." said Lawrence.

生词表

生词

1. 挑战	tiǎozhàn	challenge
2. 品尝	pǐncháng	to taste
3. 打卡	dǎ kǎ	visit a place
4. 辣	là	spicy
5. 惊讶	jīngyà	surprised
6. 臭	chòu	smelly
7. 香	xiāng	fragrant
8. 缓解	huǎnjiě	to lessen
9. 难以	nányǐ	be difficult to
10. 抗拒	kàngjù	to resist
11. 评价	píngjià	to appraise
12. 反驳	fǎnbó	to refute
13. 诱人	yòurén	attractive
14. 嚼劲	jiáojìn	chewy

成语、俗语、惯用语等

1. 天翻地覆	tiānfān-dìfù	turned upside down / huge different
2. 色香味俱全	sè xiāng wèi jù quán	having a good color, smell and taste
3. 不可思议	bùkěsīyì	inconceivable

语法点

1. 甚至……：表示一个事实或情况超出了预期范围，强调某种程度的突出或出乎意料的情况。

例句： 美国人李夏天说中文很标准，甚至还会说四川方言。

2. 即使……，也……：某种不利或困难的条件，但仍然能够实现某种结果或采取某种行动。

例句： 即使作为中国人，她也很难接受这个味道。

3. “把 +O.+V.+ 其他成分”：强调动作对宾语的处置。

例句： 把仙草、糯米丸和奶茶混合到一起。

课文结构分析

请根据这个思维导图，用完整的句子对课文进行复述。

- 一百元挑战成都小吃街
  - 地点
    - 成都建设路小吃街
  - 一百元人民币可以吃到
    - 臭豆腐
    - 火锅鸡爪
    - 鸡翅包糯米饭
    - 烧仙草
    - 芋圆冰沙
    - 煎饼
    - 脏咖啡流心蛋糕

练习

1. 根据课文内容回答下面的问题。（5 分）

（1）成都最出名的是什么？（2 分）

（2）“网红”小吃街在哪儿？

（3）李夏天夫妇在这一天要进行什么挑战？

（4）根据上下文，“吃货”的意思是什么？

2. 请把左边的词语和右边的解释对应起来。（5 分）

（1）天翻地覆 □

（2）难以接受 □

（3）反驳 □

（4）诱人 □

（5）色香味俱全 □

A. 无法忍受

B. 吸引人的

C. 非常大的差别

D. 昏天黑地

E. 风沙

F. 用自己的理由反对别人的观点

G. 耐心等待

H. 外观、香气、味道全都特别好

3. 根据课文内容判断下列说法的对错，并写出理由。（5 分） 对 错

（1）小吃街上不仅有当地人，还有外国来的游客。 □ □

理由：______________________________

（2）李夏天夫妇都非常喜欢吃各种美食。 □ □

理由：______________________________

（3）李夏天不但会说中文，还会说四川话。 □ □

理由：______________________________

（4）李夏天和他的太太都喜欢吃臭豆腐。 □ □

理由：______________________________

（5）烧仙草是中国南方地区的传统特色烧烤食物。 □ □

理由：______________________________

课文2 筷子

课前热身

请仔细观察下面这张图片，用两分钟左右的时间描述一下你在图片上看到了什么，以及你对图片的理解。

课文 2

扫一扫，看视频

筷　子

筷子是中餐桌上必备的餐具，也是东方饮食文化的标志之一，其使用可以追溯至3000多年前，其设计和使用方法也充满了文化寓意。

筷子，古称“箸”，通常由竹、木、骨、瓷等材料制作而成。为什么中国人用筷子吃饭？直接原因是中餐中有大量热食，需要借助工具来避免手指直接接触食物，更主要的原因与烹饪方式有很大关系。考古发现，距今大约7000年前中国就出现了“勺”，4000多年前就开始使用“骨制叉”，西周时期的“匕匙”可切可捞。当这些餐具的使用不能满足烹饪文化的发展时，于是就产生了筷子。中国的炒菜、火锅、面条这类烫并且小块的食物用筷子夹起来既不会烫手，又很方便。

对没有接触过筷子的人来说，用筷子吃饭简直就是一个技术活儿。我们需要用一只手握住两根筷子，通过手指灵活的协调动作才能将饭菜夹起送入口中。一旦学会使用筷子，这简单的两根筷子就会成为手指的延伸，几乎可以驾驭所有类型的食物。

对于中国人来说，简单、平凡的筷子既是不可或缺的用餐工具，也是传承千年的文化符号。传统的中式筷子都是一头圆一头方的，圆的一头象征天，方的一头象征地。“天圆地方”是古代中国人对世界的朴素理解，而用圆的一头夹取食物，则代表着“民以食为天”。筷子的名称来源于谐音字“快”，有快乐幸福之意。同时，筷子也寓意长久，如果你有亲朋好友喜结连理，你可以把筷子当作礼物送给新人。两根筷子才能成为一对，代表夫妻同心，其利断金，送十双筷子则有十全十美之意。当然，中国人在使用筷子时也有一些禁忌，比如不要把筷子竖直插进饭或菜里，也不要用筷子敲击碗或者盘子，这些都是不礼貌的行为。

有的筷子不仅是一种餐具，还是一种艺术品。中国人在筷子上题词、刻诗、绘画、烙画、镶嵌、雕镂……小小的筷子堪称中华文明的传承链，以独特的形式传承着中华民族的特色文化。

Chopsticks

As a essential tableware item of the Chinese nation and one of the symbols in Oriental diet culture, chopsticks boast a history of more than 3,000 years, which embody the Chinese wisdom in their designs and use.

Chopsticks, also known as “zhu” in ancient China, are usually made of bamboo, wood, bone, porcelain, or other materials. But why do Chinese people eat with chopsticks? First, it’s because many Chinese foods are served hot, making it necessary to use tool to avoid direct contact with the food. More importantly, it has a lot to do with cookery. Archaeological discoveries show that the spoon appeared in China about 7,000 years ago, and then came the “bone forks” over 4,000 years ago. The spoon of the Western Zhou period (1046–771 BC) was capable of cutting and scooping. When these utensils could no longer meet the requirements of the developing culinary culture, chopsticks emerged.

Chinese food which is usually served hot and in smaller pieces such as stir-fry food, hot pots, and noodles were more convenient to eat with chopsticks.

Eating with chopsticks is a real trick for first-time learners. Holding two chopsticks with one hand, you have to pick up the food and bring it to your mouth through flexible and coordinated movements of your fingers. The chopsticks, however, can become an extension of your fingers once you master the skill. They enable you to hold almost any type of food.

Though simple and ordinary, chopsticks are the essential tools for dinner and bear the inheritance of culture for the Chinese people. Traditional Chinese chopsticks are round at one end and square at the other. The round symbolizes the sky, and the square symbolizes the ground. The "round sky and square ground" is the simple understanding of the world by ancient Chinese people, while holding food with the round end represents "Food is the first necessity of the people". The name of chopsticks comes from the homophonic word "Kuai", which means happiness. At the same time, chopsticks also mean long-lasting. If you have relatives or friends who get married, you can give chopsticks as a gift to the couple. Only two chopsticks can become a pair, which means that the husband and wife are united, and they will overcome difficulties. Ten pairs of chopsticks mean be perfect in all respects. Meanwhile, there have some taboos when using chopsticks. For example, don't insert them vertically into rice or vegetables, and don't tap bowls or plates with chopsticks. These are impolite behaviors.

Chopsticks are not only an eating tool, but also a kind of art carrier.

Chopsticks can take on themselves a variety of art forms such as inscriptions, paintings, pyrography, inlays, and carvings. Small as they are, chopsticks can pass on Chinese civilization, carrying forward different forms of unique Chinese culture.

生词表

生词

1. 餐具	cānjù	tableware
2. 追溯	zhuīsù	trace back
3. 借助	jièzhù	with the help of
4. 避免	bìmiǎn	to avoid
5. 接触	jiēchù	to touch
6. 烹饪	pēngrèn	cooking
7. 考古	kǎogǔ	archaeology
8. 灵活	línghuó	flexible
9. 协调	xiétiáo	to coordinate
10. 延伸	yánshēn	to extened
11. 驾驭	jiàyù	to manage
12. 象征	xiàngzhēng	to symbolize
13. 来源	láiyuán	come from
14. 禁忌	jìnjì	taboo
15. 堪称	kānchēng	be called
16. 传承	chuánchéng	to inherit
17. 独特	dútè	unique

成语、俗语、惯用语等

1. 不可或缺	bùkěhuòquē	indispensable
2. 天圆地方	tiānyuán-dìfāng	round sky and square earth
3. 民以食为天	mín yǐ shí wéi tiān	Food is the first necessity of the people.
4. 喜结连理	xǐjié-liánlǐ	be happily married
5. 夫妻同心，其利断金	fūqī tóng xīn，qí lì duàn jīn	When husband and wife are of the same mind, their combined strength can cut through a piece of metal.
6. 十全十美	shíquán-shíměi	be perfect in all respects

语法点

1. 一旦……就……：表示条件关系的关联词。

例句： 一旦学会使用筷子，这简单的两根筷子就会成为手指的延伸。

2. 既……又……：表示并列关系，相当于又……又……。

例句： 用筷子夹起来既不会烫手，又很方便。

3. 不仅……还……：表示递进关系。

例句： 有的筷子不仅是一种餐具，还是一种艺术品。

课文结构分析

请根据这个思维导图，用完整的句子对课文进行复述。

- 筷子
  - 第一段
    - 筷子的意义
      - 中餐的餐具
      - 3000 多年历史
      - 东方饮食文化的标志
  - 第二段
    - 筷子的别名和材料
      - 古称“箸”
      - 材料：竹、木、骨、瓷
    - 使用筷子的目的
      - 避免手指直接接触食物
      - 不会烫手
      - 方便夹起小块的食物
  - 第三段
    - 筷子的使用
      - 需要手指灵活的协调动作
      - 手指的延伸
  - 第四段
    - 筷子的寓意
      - 天圆地方
      - 民以食为天
      - 快乐幸福
      - 长长久久
      - 十全十美
    - 使用筷子的禁忌
      - 把筷子竖直插进饭或菜里
      - 用筷子敲击餐具
  - 第五段
    - 特色文化
      - 在筷子上题词、刻诗、绘画、烙画、镶嵌、雕镂

练习

1. 根据课文内容，解释下列句子中画线的部分。（5 分）

（1）筷子是中餐桌上<u>必备</u>的餐具。

（2）筷子的使用可以<u>追溯</u>至 3000 多年前。

（3）……用筷子夹起来<u>既不会烫手，又很方便</u>。

（4）……<u>几乎</u>可以驾驭所有类型的食物。

（5）中国人在使用筷子时也有一些<u>禁忌</u>。

2. 根据课文内容回答下面的问题。（5 分）

（1）中国古人怎么称呼筷子？

（2）根据第②段，中餐食物有哪两个特点？（2 分）

（3）根据第③段，怎么才能很好地使用筷子？（2 分）

3. 根据课文内容，从右边选出最合适的结尾来完成左边的短句。（5 分）

（1）筷子是 □

（2）距今大约 7000 年前， □

（3）一旦学会使用筷子， □

（4）“天圆地方”是古代中国人 □

（5）筷子以独特的形式 □

A. 两根筷子就会成为手指的延伸。

B. 传承着中华民族的特色文化。

C. 堪称中华文明的传承链。

D. 东方饮食文化的标志之一。

E. 则有十全十美之意。

F. 对世界的朴素理解。

G. 中国就有“勺”的出现。

H. 将饭菜夹起送入口中。

拓展练习

话题活动

活动 A

观看视频《中华文明之美》第 178 集“筷子的历史”，了解筷子的历史。

活动 B

观看视频“如何正确使用筷子”，学习使用筷子。如果已经会使用筷子，也可以举办“筷子夹花生”的比赛。

活动 C

上网找出不同材质和不同样式的筷子的图片，然后以“筷子”为主题做一张彩色海报，并说明每种筷子的特点。

话题讨论

话题 A

同学互访，了解对方使用筷子过程中的趣事，以及吃中餐的经历。

观看视频《中国范儿》“筷子：绝没有那么简单！”了解各国不同人群对“为什么吃饭要使用筷子”的理解。然后采访一位或多位同学，收集以下信息：什么时候开始学习使用筷子的；使用筷子过程中发生的趣事和尴尬的事情；中餐厅的特点；中餐餐桌的特点和桌面设置；吃中餐时的礼仪。

话题 B

观看中央电视台公益广告“筷子篇”，思考并分享你的观点：为什么说“一双筷子里面浓缩了中国人最深邃的爱意与情感”？

写作练习

你在学习使用筷子或者品尝中国菜时发生或遇到过哪些有意思的事儿，请根据你的经历或见闻写一篇 500 ～ 700 字的文章，题目自拟。

文化点

中国药膳

中国药膳是指将中药与食材相结合，制作成具有药用价值的食物。药膳在中国有着悠久的历史和广泛的应用，被视为一种养生保健的方法，经常食用可以防病治病，保健强身，延年益寿。以下是一些常见的药膳及其功效。

当归鸡汤：当归与鸡肉炖煮而成，具有滋补血液、调理月经不调的功效。

红枣莲子糊：将红枣和莲子煮熟后磨成糊状，有益气补血、养颜美容的作用。

枸杞炖猪肝：将枸杞与猪肝炖煮，具有滋补肝脏、明目养颜的功效。

薏米山药粥：将薏米和山药煮成粥，有健脾益肾、美白养颜的功效。

当归炖鲤鱼：由当归、鲤鱼、姜片等材料炖煮而成，有补血养颜、滋阴润燥的作用。

黑豆银耳汤：由黑豆和银耳炖煮而成，有补肾养胃、润肤美容的功效。

这些药膳在中国传统医学中被认为具有调理身体、预防疾病和促进健康的功效。然而，使用药膳时需要根据个人体质和健康状况来选择合适的食材和药材，并遵循适量食用的原则，以确保安全性和有效性。

话题二 衣着

教学内容和目标	文化点
1. 了解中国人服饰搭配的特点和着装基本礼仪。 2. 了解中国人在工作、休闲、节日等场合的衣着特点，理解中国人衣着方式的多样性。 3. 了解中国少数民族服饰的特点和多样性。	职业装，节日服装，流行服装，民族头饰，中国人服装上的龙与凤

课文 1　奥运赛场上的中国时尚

课前热身

请仔细观察下面这张图片，用两分钟左右的时间描述一下你在图片上看到了什么，以及你对图片的理解。

课文 1

扫一扫，看视频

奥运赛场上的中国时尚

“人靠衣服马靠鞍”，这句中国俗语的意思是：马配上一副讲究的马鞍会显得特别骏美；人穿上一身得体的衣服则会分外精神。

在东京奥运会这样的国际性场合，服装不仅要好看，还要表达中国人的精神气质。

开幕式上，中国代表团穿的“开门红”礼服不仅颜色让人眼前一亮，细节更值得关注，例如女装纽扣牡丹纹就出自中国古代建筑的瓦当纹样。

在徐徐升起的国旗映衬下，运动员登上领奖台时所穿的衣服也是国家形象的另一种展示。中国队的领奖服由中国艺术家叶锦添设计——他当年曾凭借《卧虎藏龙》获得奥斯卡“最佳艺术指导”奖。他舍弃具象化的“龙”符号，选用了唐装圆立领一字扣和中国红代表东方的意象。

鞋子也是暗藏乾坤的：图案以文物“五星出东方利中国”的祥云瑞兽纹样为灵感；鞋身内侧包含金、木、水、火、土五行元素。

中国有一个成语叫“龙姿凤采”，用来形容人的姿态非凡出众。奥运赛场上，中国女子蹦床队的凤凰旗袍体操服也成功登上热搜。姑娘们胸前的凤凰图案表示着她们用绝美的赛场风姿夺得好成绩的决心。此外，凤凰图案也出现在场地自行车中国运动员的头盔上。

而中国乒乓球队“龙服”则继续保持原有的“龙”元素，腾飞怒吼的巨龙看起来十分有气势。

青蛇与白蛇是中国家喻户晓的民间传说。以此为元素设计的中国花样游泳队赛服图案，与花样游泳动作相呼应，表现出了缠绵灵动的美感，非常亮眼。

口罩也是本届奥运会必不可少的装备，红黄配色来自中国国旗，还增添了五角星的元素，不仅辨识度极高，也很有设计感。

服装之外，东京奥运会还有很多“硬核”的中国元素：阿里云技术支撑全球转播；山地自行车竞赛用车来自深圳……

赛场内外，中国在努力为这届“更快、更高、更强、更团结”的奥运会贡献中国力量，展示中国之美。

最后来看一个小彩蛋：本届奥运会有一支特殊的队伍——难民代表团，他们在开幕式上穿着蓝色西服出场，服装由中国品牌定制，上面绣着和平鸽的图案。愿这全人类的盛会永远展现出团结、和平、纯粹的魅力。

Chinese Fashion at the Olympic Games

The Chinese saying “People rely on clothes, and horses rely on saddles” means that a horse which is equipped with an exquisite saddle will look particularly beautiful, and a person who is appropriately dressed will be vibrant.

On such an international occasion as the Tokyo Olympic Games, the uniforms of Chinese athletes should not only be eye-catching, but also express the aspirations of the Chinese people.

At the opening ceremony of the 2020 Olympic Games, the Chinese delegation dressed in red with warm hues that conveyed the theme of "making a good start". The dress has richly carved details borrowed from Chinese culture. For instance, the peony pattern on the buttons of women's dress originates from the eaves tile pattern of ancient Chinese architecture.

Against the backdrop of the slowly hoisted national flag, the uniform worn by an athlete on the podium displayed the image of the country. The uniforms worn by the Chinese delegation to receive awards on the podium were designed by Chinese artist Tim Yip, who won an Academy Award for Best Art Director for the film *Crouching Tiger, Hidden Dragon*. He abandoned the "dragon" symbol and chose images to represent the East — the round stand-up collar of Tang suit, cross buckle, and red — an auspicious color in Chinese culture.

The shoes also carried an enchanting element. The design of shoes was inspired by the auspicious cloud and beast pattern from the cultural relic "five stars come out of the East and benefit China", and the inside of the shoes contained five elements: metal, wood, water, fire, and earth.

The Chinese idiom "figure of dragon and phoenix" is used to describe a person's extraordinary posture. At the Olympic Games, the phoenix cheongsam gymnastic uniforms of the Chinese women's trampoline team were also a trending topic on social media. The phoenix pattern on the chest indicated their determination to receive awards with their extraordinary posture. It also appears on the helmets of Chinese cyclists.

The Chinese table tennis team has a roaring dragon splashed on its uniform which looks imposing.

In Chinese folklore, the Green Snake and the White Snake are well-known. The Chinese synchronized swimming team's uniform displayed patterns from their tales. During synchronized swimming movements, the slithering curves showed an eye-catching agile beauty.

Masks were also essential accessories for the Tokyo Olympic Games. The red and yellow colors originated from the Chinese national flag, and the element of the five-star pattern was added, which was not only highly recognizable, but also well-designed.

Apart from uniforms, there were other Chinese elements in the Tokyo Olympic Games. The global broadcasting was supported by Alibaba Cloud technology, and the mountain bike racing vehicles came from Shenzhen....

Both inside and outside of the stadium, China was making efforts to contribute to a faster, higher, stronger, and more united Olympic Games while showcasing the country's beauty.

There was a heart-warming moment at the Olympic Games. A special team — the Refugee Olympic Team paraded into the stadium at the opening ceremony. Its members appeared in blue suits, which are customized by Chinese brands and embroidered with the pattern of peace doves. May this grand gathering of all mankind always show unity, peace, and purity.

生词表

生词

1. 讲究	jiǎngjiu	exquisite
2. 得体	détǐ	decent
3. 分外	fènwài	particularly
4. 值得	zhídé	be worth
5. 领奖台	lǐngjiǎngtái	podium
6. 舍弃	shěqì	give up
7. 意象	yìxiàng	image
8. 元素	yuánsù	element
9. 灵感	línggǎn	inspiration
10. 凤凰	fènghuáng	phoenix
11. 头盔	tóukuī	helmet
12. 辨识度	biànshídù	recognizable
13. 硬核	yìnghé	hardcore
14. 彩蛋	cǎidàn	post credits
15. 难民	nànmín	refugee
16. 魅力	mèilì	charm

成语、俗语、惯用语等

1. 人靠衣服马靠鞍	rén kào yīfu mǎ kào ān	Clothes make the man; fine feathers make fine birds.
2. 眼前一亮	yǎnqiányíliàng	look stunning
3. 暗藏乾坤	àncáng-qiánkūn	carry a surprise element
4. 家喻户晓	jiāyù-hùxiǎo	be known to every houshold

语法点

并列词组：由两个或两个以上的名词、动词、形容词、代词或数量词等组合而成，词与词之间是并列关系，中间常用顿号。

例句： 更快、更高、更强、更团结

课文结构分析

请根据这个思维导图，用完整的句子对课文进行复述。

- 奥运赛场上的中国时尚
  - 服装的作用
    - 人靠衣服马靠鞍
    - 表示精神气质
  - 开幕式中国队服
    - “开门红”礼服
    - 女装纽扣牡丹纹
  - 中国队的领奖服
    - 唐装圆立领
    - 一字扣
    - 中国红
  - 鞋子
    - 灵感：祥云瑞兽纹样
    - 内侧：金、木、水、火、土五行元素
  - 凤凰图案
    - 女子蹦床队　凤凰旗袍体操服
    - 场地自行车队　头盔
  - 龙元素
    - 中国乒乓球队
    - 有气势
  - 蛇元素
    - 花样游泳队服
    - 灵感：青蛇与白蛇的民间传说
  - 口罩
    - 红黄配色：中国国旗
    - 五角星
  - 科技
    - 阿里云技术：传播赛事

练习

1. 根据课文内容回答下面的问题。(10 分)

（1）马为什么需要佩戴精美的马鞍？（1 分）

（2）中国代表团开幕式队服有什么值得关注的细节？（1 分）

（3）中国代表团的领奖服是由谁设计的？这个人有过什么成就？（2 分）

（4）中国运动员的鞋子的设计灵感是什么？（2 分）

（5）成语“龙姿凤采”是什么意思？（1 分）

（6）中国女子蹦床队的体操服上有什么图案？为什么要有这样的设计？（2 分）

（7）请在第⑧段找出一个代表女子花样游泳优美动作的词语。（1 分）

2. 根据课文内容，从右边选出最合适的结尾来完成左边的短句。（5 分）

（1）服装不仅要好看， □

（2）运动员的领奖服 □

（3）腾飞怒吼的巨龙 □

（4）中国队的口罩不仅辨识度极高， □

（5）愿这全人类的盛会 □

A. 也很有设计感。

B. 细节值得关注。

C. 永远展现出团结、和平、纯粹的魅力。

D. 也是国家形象的另一种展示。

E. 还要表达中国人的精神气质。

F. 出自中国古代建筑的瓦当纹样。

G. 看起来十分有气势。

课文 2　苗族银饰

课前热身

请仔细观察下面这张图片，用两分钟左右的时间描述一下你在图片上看到了什么，以及你对图片的理解。

课文 2

扫一扫，看视频

苗族银饰

2016 年 4 月，一部名为《走进贵州苗寨》的纪录片刷爆了法国人的社交网络，首播吸引了超过 500 万法国人在电视机前观看。这部纪录片讲述的是居住在中国西南部村寨的少数民族——苗族的生活，其中“会走路就会跳舞，会说话就会唱歌”的苗族姑娘打动了许多观众。其实，苗族姑娘不仅能歌善舞，她们的节日盛装上那满身的银饰也非常引人瞩目。

苗族姑娘为何钟爱银饰？这要从苗族的历史说起。相传在古代，苗族人曾聚居于长江中下游及黄河流域一带，为了躲避长年的战争，全民族进行了数次大迁徙，最后定居在中国的西南地区。在迁徙过程中，苗族人把家产换成银子，打造成银器方便戴在身上。他们认为银器可以辟邪，还能去毒，让家人远离灾难。如今，苗族人已经过上安居乐业的生活，但银饰依旧是他们生活中不可或缺的一部分。每逢节日庆典、婚姻嫁娶的重要时刻，苗族姑娘就会从头到脚穿戴上银角、银链、银圈、银衣、银镯等银饰。这一身行头少则七八斤，多则二三十斤。但苗族姑娘并不觉得沉重，她们认为这是自己最美的时刻。

银饰的造型和图案展示了苗族人的图腾崇拜。银角是苗族人最重要的银饰之一。它犹如一对伸展的大水牛角，高度几乎是佩戴者身高的一半。这个奇特的造型源自苗族祖先蚩尤的形象，意在纪念祖先，希望获得其保佑。除了蚩尤，苗族人把蝴蝶尊称为“蝴蝶妈妈”，把枫树看作是神树。所以，蝴蝶和枫树也是苗族银饰里最常见的图案。由于大迁徙，苗族人的文字逐渐丢失，除了山歌和口口相传，他们还通过服装上的刺绣、银饰图案来传承自己的历史文化，所以银饰被称为苗族“穿在身上的史诗”。

苗族姑娘美丽的银饰少不了银匠手艺的巧夺天工。苗族银饰锻制工艺是世代相传的，银饰的加工过程全靠手工，因而工匠练就了高超的技艺，甚至能拉出比头发丝还细的银丝，每一件银饰都是独一无二的精工之作。正因如此，苗族银饰手工锻制技艺已于2006年被列入了中国非物质文化遗产保护名录，并被列为三十项濒危非物质文化遗产之一。

经过祖祖辈辈的积累和流传，许多苗族姑娘都拥有一套自己的银饰。她们头饰上的银片颤动发出的沙沙声、胸前项圈的叮当撞击声是节日里必不可少的音乐。银饰不仅仅是单纯的工艺品，还是苗族历史文化的印记，更凝聚了苗族的民族灵魂。

Miao Silver Ornaments

In April 2016, the documentary “Into the Miao Village in Guizhou Province” went viral on French social media, attracting more than five million French viewers. The documentary is about the life of Miao ethnic group living in villages in southwest China, and the Miao girls who “can dance and sing" impressed many viewers. In fact, the Miao girls are not only good at singing and dancing, their festival costumes covered with silver ornaments are also very eye-catching.

Why do Miao girls love silver ornaments? This starts with the history of the Miao ethnic group. Legend has it that in ancient times, the Miao people once lived in the middle and lower reaches of the Yangtze River and the Yellow River basin. In order to avoid the years of wars, the whole group made several great migrations and finally settled in the southwest of China. During the migration, the Miao people changed their property into silver ornaments to wear on. They believe that silver can ward off evil and poison, keep families away from disaster. Today, the Miao people have lived a happy and peaceful life, but silver jewelry is still an indispensable decoration of their lives. During the important moments of festivals and marriages, the Miao girls will wear silver ornaments such as silver horns, chains, rings, clothes, and bracelets from head to toe. The outfits can weigh seven or eight *jin* to over 20 or 30. But the Miao girls do not feel onerous. They think this is their most beautiful moment.

The shape and pattern of the silver ornaments show the totem worship of the Miao people. Silver horn is one of the most important silver ornaments. It is like a pair of outstretched large buffalo horns, almost half the wearer's height. This shape comes from the image of Chiyou, the Miao ancestor, and is intended to commemorate the ancestors in the hope of obtaining their blessing. In addition to Chiyou, the Miao people called the butterfly "mother butterfly" and considered the maple tree as a sacred tree. Therefore, butterflies and maple trees are also the most common patterns in Miao silver ornaments. Due to the great migration, the Miao people's characters are gradually lost. In addition to folk songs and oral biographies, they also inherit their history and culture through embroidery and silver ornaments on their costumes. Therefore, silver ornaments are called the "epic worn on the body" of the Miao people.

The beautiful silver ornaments of the Miao girls are made by the silvers craftmen who possess the superb craftsmanship. The forging technology of Miao silver ornaments is handed down from generation to generation. The processing of making silver ornaments is by hand, so they have practiced superb skills, and even can pull out the thinner silver silk than the hair, making each piece of silver a unique fine artwork. Because of this, the Miao silver forging technique has been listed in China's intangible cultural heritage protection list in 2006 and has been listed as one of the 30 endangered intangible cultural heritages.

After generations of accumulation and inheritance, many Miao girls have a set of their own silver ornaments. The rustling of the silver pieces on their headdress and the jingle of their chest collars were the festival music. A silver ornament is not only a simple handicraft, but also the mark of the history and culture of the Miao ethnic group and embodies the soul of the Miao people.

生词表

生词

1. 钟爱	zhōng'ài	to cherish
2. 聚居	jùjū	live in a compact community
3. 流域	liúyù	drainage basin
4. 躲避	duǒbì	to avoid
5. 迁徙	qiānxǐ	to migrate
6. 辟邪	bìxié	ward off/exorcise evil spirits
7. 佩戴	pèidài	to wear
8. 刺绣	cìxiù	embroidery
9. 颤动	chàndòng	to shake
10. 凝聚	níngjù	to condense
11. 灵魂	línghún	soul

成语、俗语、惯用语等

1. 能歌善舞	nénggē-shànwǔ	be good at singing and dancing
2. 引人瞩目	yǐnrén-zhǔmù	eye-catching
3. 安居乐业	ānjū-lèyè	live and work in peace
4. 图腾崇拜	túténg chóngbài	totem worship
5. 巧夺天工	qiǎoduó-tiāngōng	ingenious workmanship
6. 世代相传	shìdài xiāngchuán	pass down from generation to generation
7. 独一无二	dúyī-wú'èr	unique
8. 必不可少	bìbùkěshǎo	essential

语法点

1. 设问句：无疑而问，自问自答，以引导读者注意和思考问题。

例句： 苗族姑娘为何钟爱银饰？这要从苗族的历史说起。

2. 通过：以人或事物为媒介或手段而达到某种目的。

例句： 苗族通过服装上的刺绣、银饰图案来传承自己的历史文化。

课文结构分析

请根据这个思维导图，用完整的句子对课文进行复述。

- 苗族银饰
  - 苗族的历史
    - 躲避战争，数次迁徙
    - 把家产换成银子
    - 把银子打造成银器
    - （银器可以辟邪，远离灾难）
  - 服饰
    - 节日庆典
    - 婚姻嫁娶
    - （从头到脚穿戴上银角、银链、银圈、银衣、银镯）
  - 银饰的造型和图案
    - 展示了苗族人的图腾崇拜
      - 苗族祖先蚩尤
      - 蝴蝶
      - 枫树
  - 苗族银饰
    - 重量：少则七八斤，多则二三十斤
    - 意义
      - 苗族历史文化的印记
      - 苗族的民族灵魂
  - 银匠手艺
    - 列入中国非物质文化遗产保护名录
    - 列为三十项濒危非物质文化遗产之一

练习

1. 根据课文内容，选出五个正确的表述。(5 分)

☐ A.《走进贵州苗寨》是一部讲述苗族生活的故事片。

B. 苗族姑娘在学会走路之前先学习跳舞。

☐ C. 一部分苗族人很久以前聚居在长江中下游地区。

D. 苗族人因为不停地搬家，所以需要把家产换成银子，再打造成银器戴在身上。

☐ E. 苗族姑娘头上戴的银角重达二三十斤。

☐ F. 苗族姑娘戴的银角就像一对伸展的大水牛角。

G. 苗族银饰里最常见的图案包括蝴蝶和枫树。

☐ H. 制作苗族银饰的银匠手艺超群。

2. 根据课文内容回答下面的问题。（5 分）

（1）苗族人通过什么来传承自己的历史文化？（2 分）

（2）苗族银饰是怎么加工制造的？（1 分）

（3）在课文的第⑤段“是节日里必不可少的音乐”，这里的“音乐”指的是什么？（2分）

3. 根据课文内容，从右边选出最合适的结尾来完成左边的短句。（5 分）

（1）苗族姑娘身上戴的银饰	☐	A. 不可或缺的一部分。
		B. 也非常引人瞩目。
（2）为了躲避长年的战争	☐	C. 更凝聚了苗族的民族灵魂。
		D. 全民族进行了数次大迁徙。
（3）银饰依旧是他们生活中	☐	E. 佩戴者身高的一半。
（4）银角的高度几乎是	☐	F. 定居在中国的西南地区。
		G. 过上安居乐业的生活。
（5）银饰是苗族历史文化的印记，	☐	H. 是自己最美的时刻。

拓展练习

话题活动

活动 A

请为你的学校设计校服，并说明你的设计理念。

活动 B

通过上网搜集资料了解中国传统服饰中常用的颜色和纹饰，它们有什么象征意义或故事，请给您的同学讲一讲。

活动 C

学唱歌曲《龙的传人》或朗诵歌词，在班级进行表演或比赛。

话题讨论

分组讨论：上网查看有关中国人的服饰变化的资料，讨论中国人衣着风格的变化与时代的关系。

写作练习

假如你是一位服装设计师，要设计一套衣服参加春节庆祝活动。请你以“文化融合”为理念来设计这套衣服，并用 500 ～ 700 字谈谈你的设计想法。

文化点

祥云纹

祥云纹作为中国传统的吉祥纹饰，其实是古代云纹的一种演变。古时候，人们对于“天界”和“神”特别向往，总想知道云之上有什么。出于对云的敬畏和崇拜，人们把云纹绣在衣服上或者刻在饰品上，后来慢慢衍生出各种和云有关的纹饰。云纹便成了中国传统图案中人们喜闻乐见的图案。汉语里有“平步青云”这样的成语，寓意“高升”，又因云纹形似如意而被赋予了吉祥的寓意。云纹这一“简单”的图案纹饰，经过几千年的发展演变，其本体得到不断地丰富。每个历史时期的云纹样式都融入各自时代的不同风貌。中国云纹艺术也因此显出它的博大精深，散发着无限的魅力。

话题三 休闲

教学内容和目标	文化点
1. 了解中国人休闲娱乐活动的特点。 2. 了解中国人休闲方式的多样性。 3. 了解中国传统体育活动，如武术、太极拳等的特点和文化含义。	武术，太极拳

课文 1　冰嬉

课前热身

请仔细观察下面这张图片，用两分钟左右的时间描述一下你在图片上看到了什么，以及你对图片的理解。

课文 1

扫一扫，看视频

冰　嬉

“冰嬉”是中国古代各项冰上活动的统称，起源于宋朝，在清朝时期达到鼎盛，多出现于冬季的中国北方地区。

清朝时期，冰嬉作为一项国家军事活动而开展。士兵们穿上特制的冰鞋在冰面上训练和表演各种高难度动作，既是一种娱乐方式，也可以提高作战灵活性与抗寒能力。冬至过后，皇帝会在北海公园举行隆重的冰嬉盛典。盛典上除了进行冰上歌舞表演外，还会开展各项冰上竞技体育活动，“抢灯”“抢球”“转龙射球”都是经典项目，相当于如今体育赛场上的速滑、橄榄球、花样杂技等竞技比赛。2019 年，北京故宫举办了“紫禁城里过大年”展览，展览上展出了乾隆皇帝时期宫廷画家张为邦、姚文翰所绘的《冰嬉图》，这幅画表现的就是当时宫廷冰上表演的盛况。

时至今日，冰嬉这项传统的冰上活动被保留下来，延续着时代的印记。每年冬至，北海公园都会举行皇家冰嬉表演，冰嬉表演队员身着八旗士兵的服饰、脚踏冰鞋进行演出，表演动作多来自《冰嬉图》记载的经典冰上动作，再现当年的盛况。

中国民间的冰上活动也十分丰富。在北京，每逢深冬，散落在京城大大小小的冰场就会迎来一年中最热闹的时刻。什刹海、颐和园等地都有老少云集的戏冰场所，这一景象被无数的文学、影视作品提及或展示，成为北京人冬日记忆中最难忘的一部分。

Chinese Ice Game —Ice Frolicking

Ice frolicking is an umbrella term for various ice activities in ancient China. It originated in the Song Dynasty (960-1279), reached its peak in the Qing Dynasty (1616-1911), and was popular in northern China in winter.

During the Qing Dynasty, ice frolicking became a national military activity. Soldiers put on ice shoes to train and perform various difficult movements on the ice, which was not only a recreation but also a way to temper soldiers' combat flexibility and resistance to cold. After the Winter Solstice, the emperor would hold a grand ice frolicking ceremony in Beihai Park. In addition to singing and dancing performances on the ice, ice sports competitions were held. The classic events included "grabbing the lantern and the ball, turning the dragon and shooting the ball", which are equivalent to speed skating, football, acrobatics, and other competitions. In 2019, the Forbidden City held an exhibition on the theme of Celebrating Spring Festival. In this exhibition, the painting *Ice Frolicking* by court painters Zhang Weibang and Yao Wenhan during the reign of Emperor Qianlong was displayed. It was based on the grand performances of the courtiers on the ice at that time.

So far, the traditional activity of ice frolicking has been preserved. Every Winter Solstice, Beihai Park holds a royal ice frolicking performance. The ice frolicking performers wear clothes similar to those worn by Eight Banners soldiers during the Qing Dynasty and perform in ice shoes. Most of the performances are based on classic ice movements recorded in the *Ice Frolicking* painting to reproduce the grand occasion at that time.

Chinese folk ice activities are also very popular. In Beijing, every winter, the ice rinks scattered in the capital, big or small, are busiest. In Shichahai, Summer Palace and other places, people gather for ice frolicking. This scene has been mentioned by many literary, film, and TV works and has become an unforgettable part of winter memories for those living in Beijing.

生词表

生词

1. 冰嬉	bīngxī	ice frolicking
2. 统称	tǒngchēng	general term
3. 鼎盛	dǐngshèng	peak
4. 军事	jūnshì	military affairs
5. 高难度	gāo nándù	highly diffcult
6. 灵活性	línghuóxìng	flexibility
7. 冬至	dōngzhì	Winter Solstice
8. 隆重	lóngzhòng	grand
9. 盛典	shèngdiǎn	grand ceremony

10. 宫廷	gōngtíng	court
11. 速滑	sùhuá	speed skating
12. 橄榄球	gǎnlǎnqiú	rugby (football)
13. 花样杂技	huāyàng zájì	pattern acrobatics
14. 竞技	jìngjì	competition
15. 盛况	shèngkuàng	grand occasion
16. 延续	yánxù	to continue
17. 印记	yìnjì	mark

成语、俗语、惯用语等

1. 时至今日	shízhì-jīnrì	to this day
2. 老少云集	lǎoshào yúnjí	gather young and old

语法点

除了……，还……：表示排除已经知道的，补充说明其他的。

例句：冰嬉盛典除了进行冰上歌舞表演外，还会开展各项冰上竞技体育活动。

课文结构分析

请根据这个思维导图，用完整的句子对课文进行复述。

- 冰嬉
  - 第一段
    - 起源：宋朝
    - 鼎盛：清朝
    - 季节：冬季
    - 地区：中国北方
  - 第二段
    - 国家军事活动
      - 提高作战灵活性
      - 提高抗寒能力
    - 宫廷冰嬉盛典
      - 冰上歌舞表演
      - 冰上竞技体育活动
      - 冰嬉图
  - 第三段
    - 传统活动
      - 时间：冬至
      - 地点：北海公园
      - 皇家冰嬉表演
  - 第四段
    - 中国民间冰上活动
      - 什刹海
      - 颐和园

练习

1. 根据课文内容，选出五个正确的表述。(5 分)

□ A.“冰嬉”起源于宋朝。

B. 清朝的时候，军人们要穿上冰鞋进行“冰嬉”。

□ C. 皇家冰嬉盛典一般在冬至前举行。

D.“抢灯”“抢球”“转龙射球”相当于速滑、橄榄球、花样杂技竞技赛。

□ E.《冰嬉图》于 2019 年在北京故宫展出。

□ F. 在冬天，北京有很多让人们滑冰的场地。

G. 在清朝，冰嬉作为一项娱乐活动而开展。

□ H. 每年冬至，北海公园都会举行冰嬉表演。

2. 根据课文内容回答下面的问题。（5 分）

（1）古代的军事冰嬉活动有哪些目的？请举两个例子。（2 分）

（2）《冰嬉图》表现了什么场景？（1 分）

（3）现在的冰嬉表演队员要穿什么样的衣服进行表演？（2 分）

3. 根据课文内容，把左边的词语和右边的解释对应起来。（5 分）

（1）鼎盛	□	A. 很大很热闹的情景
		B. 冬天最冷的一段时间
（2）盛典	□	C. 最强盛
		D. 冬季里的一个节气
（3）盛况	□	E. 有非常好的名声
		F. 盛大的仪式
（4）深冬	□	G. 规模很大
（5）冬至	□	H. 冬天冰天雪地的情景

课文 2　太极拳

课前热身

请仔细观察下面这张图片，用两分钟左右的时间描述一下你在图片上看到了什么，以及你对图片的理解。

课文 2

扫一扫，看视频

太极拳

2020 年 12 月 17 日，“太极拳”被列入联合国教科文组织非物质文化遗产名录。太极拳是中国古代武术的一种，形成于 17 世纪中叶，到今天已经传承了 300 多年。它是中华民族辩证思维与武术、艺术、中医等的完美结合。

太极讲究阴阳循环、天人合一。太极拳也基于同样的思想，要求练拳之人立身要中正，动作要松柔圆活，一招一式尽显刚柔并济之美，一动一静尽展中国功夫气韵。经过多年的发展，太极拳还融入了中国传统儒家价值观念，例如尊师重道，不可不敬、不可狂、不可满等，体现了“和”的理念。

将拳术的形体运动与中医学相结合是太极拳的精髓所在。太极拳通过动作平衡肌肉和关节，巧妙运用腹部呼吸，保证形体运动不妨碍人体的肺脏呼吸运动，从而达到治病健身的效果。新冠肺炎疫情发生后，太极拳“提高免疫力”和“改善气血和肺功能”的抗疫价值得到凸显，钟南山和张伯礼院士对此也给予了充分肯定。

练太极拳既能放松肢体又能静心，长期练习可以帮助摆脱身体亚健康，提高生活质量。作为传统的有氧运动，太极拳动静结合，适合不同年龄的人群，甚至很多年轻人也十分青睐这项运动。

2008 年北京奥运会上，太极拳作为表演项目向世界展示；2012 年，在天宫一号上，宇航员刘洋打起太极拳；2016年，G20杭州峰会文艺晚会上，白衣翩翩的太极拳舞者在夜幕下涉水而来。

如今，太极拳已传播到全球150多个国家和地区，太极拳学习者有4亿多人，成为一项风靡全球的国际化健身形式。越来越多的外国人通过练习太极拳感受中国文化的魅力。太极拳已经成为连接不同种族、不同民族、不同语言、不同国家的文化纽带。

Taijiquan

On December 17, 2020, China's taijiquan, also know as, tai chi was included in the UNESCO Intangible Cultural Heritage List. As a kind of the ancient Chinese martial arts, it came into being in the 17th century, and has been handed down for more than 300 years. It is a perfect combination of the dialectical philosophy of the Chinese nation with martial arts, art, and traditional Chinese medicine.

Tai chi stresses the cycle of yin and yang and the unity of man and nature. Based on this thought, tai chi requires its practitioners to stand in an upright and balanced seated posture and move in a supple and smooth way. While its distinctive movement poses show the beautiful blend of strength and softness, its motions and meditative stillness display the charm of Chinese kung fu. Traditional Chinese Confucian values, such as honoring teachers and respecting rules, being humble but not being arrogant and complacent, are integrated into tai chi, which reflects the concept of harmony.

Tai chi combines the body movements of boxing with traditional Chinese medicine. It balances muscles and joints through movements and skillfully uses abdominal breathing to ensure that body movements do not hinder respiratory movements but achieve the effect of curing diseases and keeping healthy. After the outbreak of COVID-19, tai chi plays a significant role in "enhancing immunity" and "improving *qi* and blood and lung function". This has been affirmed by academicians Zhong Nanshan and Zhang Boli.

Practicing tai chi can relax not only the body but also the mind. Long-term practice can help get rid of sub-health and improve the quality of life. As a traditional aerobic exercise, tai chi combines movement and stillness and is suitable for people of all ages, with young people also enjoying the practice.

In 2008 Beijing Olympic Games, it became a performance event; in 2012, astronaut Liu Yang practiced it on "Tiangong-1"; in 2016, at the evening party of G20 Hangzhou Summit, dancers in white waded through the water at night and incorporated tai chi in their dance.

Today, tai chi has spread to over 150 countries and regions with more than 400 million practitioners, and it has become an international fitness exercise that is popular in the world. By practicing tai chi, more and more non-Chinese know about the charm of Chinese culture, and tai chi has become a cultural bond connecting different races, ethnic groups, languages and countries.

生词表

生词

1. 遗产	yíchǎn	heritage
2. 辩证	biànzhèng	dialectical
3. 思维	sīwéi	thinking
4. 气韵	qìyùn	spirit, carriage
5. 儒家	rújiā	Confucianism
6. 理念	lǐniàn	idea
7. 中医学	Zhōngyīxué	Traditional Chinese Medicine
8. 精髓	jīngsuǐ	essence
9. 妨碍	fáng'ài	to hinder
10. 凸显	tūxiǎn	prominent
11. 亚健康	yàjiànkāng	sub-health
12. 青睐	qīnglài	favor
13. 风靡	fēngmǐ	be fashionable
14. 纽带	niǔdài	link

成语、俗语、惯用语等

1. 天人合一	tiānrén-héyī	the unity of heaven and human
2. 立身中正	lìshēn zhōngzhèng	stand upright
3. 刚柔并济	gāngróu-bìngjì	blend of strength and softness
4. 尊师重道	zūnshī-zhòngdào	honoring teachers and respecting rules

语法点

1. 基于：根据。

例句：太极拳也基于同样的思想，要求练拳之人立身要中正，动作要松柔圆活。

2. 从而：连词，上文是原因、方法等，下文是结果、目的等。

例句：太极拳通过动作平衡肌肉和关节，巧妙运用腹部呼吸，保证形体运动不妨碍人体的肺脏呼吸运动，从而达到治病健身的效果。

课文结构分析

请根据这个思维导图，用完整的句子对课文进行复述。

- 太极拳
  - 第一段：太极拳的历史
    - 中国武术的一部分
    - 形成于 17 世纪中叶
    - 300 多年历史
    - 2020 年列入非物质文化遗产名录
  - 第二段：太极拳的特点
    - 结合了武术、艺术、中医等
    - 具有哲学思想
    - 儒家价值观念
    - 体现“和”的理念
    - 阴阳循环、天人合一
    - 刚柔并济
  - 第三段：太极拳可以治病健身
    - 与中医学结合
    - 平衡肌肉和关节
    - 提高免疫力
    - 改善气血和肺功能
  - 第四段：太极拳提高生活质量
    - 放松肢体
    - 静心
    - 摆脱身体亚健康
    - 适合不同年龄的人群
  - 第五段：太极拳是中华民族的文化符号
    - 2008 年北京奥运会
    - 2012 年天宫一号
    - 2016 年 G20 杭州峰会
  - 第六段：太极拳是文化纽带
    - 传播到全球 150 多个国家和地区
    - 全球 4 亿多人学习太极拳
    - 通过太极拳感受中国文化

练习

1. 根据课文内容选择正确答案。(5 分)

(1) 太极拳是 ________。 □

A. 中国现代体育运动

B. 中国传统球类运动

C. 中国传统武术的一种

D. 中国现代武术的一种

(2) 太极拳流传至今，已经 ________。 □

A. 超过 300 年

B. 不到 300 年

C.300 年左右

D. 差不多 300 年

(3) 太极拳的动作有什么特征? □

A. 非常温柔

B. 不具有力量

C. 画出圆形

D. 既柔和缓慢又带有力量

(4) 第二段最后一句中，“和”的意思是什么? □

A. 与

B. 加在一起

C. 和谐

D. 和解

(5) 太极拳在 2008 年北京奥运会上 ________。 □

A. 属于表演项目

B. 属于比赛项目

C. 白衣翩翩，涉水而来

D. 由宇航员刘洋表演

2. 根据课文内容判断下列说法的对错，并写出理由。（5 分）

	对	错
（1）太极拳 20 世纪被列入联合国教科文组织非物质文化遗产名录。	□	□
理由：______________________________		
（2）太极拳包含了中国传统的儒家思想。	□	□
理由：______________________________		
（3）太极拳可以用来治疗疾病。	□	□
理由：______________________________		
（4）太极拳是老年人的运动。	□	□
理由：______________________________		
（5）全世界有超过 4 亿人在学习太极拳。	□	□
理由：______________________________		

3. 用课文中的词语填空。（5 分）

（1）太极拳由一代又一代的人 ______ 了下来。

（2）孔子的教育______是因材施教。

（3）他的身体失去了______，一头摔倒在地上。

（4）这部手机受到了很多年轻人的______。

（5）这种病毒______的速度非常快。

4. 写出五个你知道的中国传统体育项目并上网找出与之对应的图片。

体育项目	图片
太极拳	

拓展练习

话题活动

活动 A

1. 观看电影《太极张三丰》，直观地了解太极拳刚柔并济的特点。
2. 跟着视频学习太极拳的基本动作，体会打太极拳的乐趣。

活动 B

采访太极拳师傅，了解太极拳的不同套路、太极拳的特点、太极拳的核心理念、太极拳对健康的好处、太极拳的传承和传播。

话题讨论

观看电影《推手》，并讨论：“推手”是什么意思？为什么导演以“推手”为电影的名字？电影中反映了哪些东西方文化的冲突与融合？

写作练习

很多青少年都以某位体育运动员作为自己的偶像，在成长的道路上激励自己，请用 500 ～ 700 字给你的朋友写一封信，来谈谈你的运动员偶像，题目自拟。

文化点

中国传统体育项目

中国传统体育项目有太极拳、武术（功夫）、踢毽子、中国式摔跤、中国象棋、围棋等。这些项目在中国有着悠久的历史，代表了中国人民对身体健康、心理健康和社交活动的追求。

太极拳：以柔和流畅的动作、呼吸和内功为特点的一种武术运动。它注重身体的平衡、柔韧性和内外协调，被广泛用于健身、养生领域。

武术：中国传统的格斗技艺，包括拳术、刀术、剑术、棍术等。武术注重技击技巧、身体素质和精神修养，有强身健体和自我防卫的作用。

踢毽子：一种传统的中国民间体育活动，参与者使用脚去踢毽子，展示技巧和灵活性。这项活动既有趣又有益于身体协调和灵敏度的培养。

这些中国传统体育项目在百姓的日常生活中扮演着重要角色。许多人把这些传统体育项目作为增强身体素质、保持活力并与他人分享乐趣的方式。不仅如此，这些传统体育项目还是传承和弘扬中国文化的重要形式。

话题四 出行

教学内容和目标	文化点
1. 了解中国人使用公共交通工具的基本情况。 2. 理解中国高铁和共享单车的特点以及它们对中国人出行的意义。	轨道交通，高铁，共享单车，交通治理

课文 1　中国高铁上的外卖

课前热身

请仔细观察下面这张图片，用两分钟左右的时间描述一下你在图片上看到了什么，以及你对图片的理解。

课文1

扫一扫，看视频

中国高铁上的外卖

众所周知，随着互联网的发展，人们的生活变得越来越便捷，使用手机APP点外卖已经成为大家日常生活的一部分。但你是否尝试过在中国的高铁上点外卖？你甚至很难想象在高铁上点的外卖是如何送到自己手中的吧？

阿福是一位来自德国的小伙子，目前生活在上海。听说高铁上可以点外卖了，他非常好奇。于是，他决定趁去广州出差的机会，试一试在高铁上点外卖，记录自己在中国的新经历。

出差这天，他一到候车大厅就迫不及待地打开手机APP操作起来。外卖平台上显示可点的套餐种类很多，点单的方式和平时在家点外卖差不多，配送费也并没有因为是高铁外卖而变得更贵。阿福兴奋地浏览了一遍菜单后，最终决定点两个外卖：11点04分抵达南昌时选择一份37元的香辣啤酒鸭套餐，12点28分到达长沙时来一份47元的帕尼尼套餐。按照阿福的说法，他要体验高铁在不同地区短暂停站时，外卖小哥是否真的能如期送来外卖。点好外卖后，阿福忍不住想：会不会是外卖小哥骑着电瓶车到站台来送餐？

火车抵达南昌了。阿福望见站台上有一名年轻小伙子拎着一个白色的小箱子。阿福想：那一定是我的外卖！ 可是他等啊等，一直等到火车启动，也没看到外卖小哥来给他送餐。外卖去哪里了呢？高铁上点外卖靠谱吗？

情急之下，阿福询问了车厢里的服务员。服务员告诉阿福，点好的外卖会由餐车统一送到订餐者的座位上。在服务员的帮助下，阿福终于拿到了自己点的香辣啤酒鸭套餐。这份外卖套餐和平时在家点的没有什么区别，比如，外卖的包装完好，没有渗漏。阿福打开餐盒，鸭肉、茄子、蒸蛋等菜还是热气腾腾的。阿福迫不及待地吃了几口，满意地点点头。

火车到达长沙。阿福在等待第二份外卖时就显得老练多了。他不再像之前那样焦急，而是耐心地等待服务员将外卖送到他的座位上。第二份外卖——帕尼尼的味道也很不错。

不到七个小时，阿福就顺利地从上海到达广州了。对于这次在高铁上点外卖的经历，阿福觉得还是很不错的，因为外卖的种类比高铁上的盒饭多，而且还能送到座位上，整个过程也特别方便，给他带来了很好的体验。

近年来，中国互联网科技日新月异，中国高铁高速发展，二者的结合使得高铁外卖变成了可能。自 2017 年 7 月 17 日开始，旅客们可以在高铁上点自己喜欢的外卖餐饮。2020 年，中国 100 万以上人口的城市中 94.7% 已经被高铁网覆盖。不仅仅是中国长三角、珠三角、环渤海等经济发达的地区有高铁，四川盆地、云贵高原以及甘肃、新疆等西部地区也有高铁。截止 2021 年 12 月底，中国的高铁营运里程突破 4 万公里，位居全球首位。中国高铁为人们的出行提供了便利，也为人们的出行提供了更多的选择。

Ordering Takeout on China's High-Speed Train

As many may know, the development of the internet makes ordering takeout via mobile phone apps fairly convenient in China. This has become part of people's lives. But have you ever done this while traveling on a high-speed train? Is it hard to imagine how takeout can be delivered to you?

Thomas, Chinese name Afu, who lives in Shanghai with his family, is from Germany. Though Thomas often heard about ordering takeout on a high-speed train, he had no experience and was curious about this. This time, he would try it on a business trip to Guangzhou and record this new experience in China.

On that day, as soon as he got to the waiting hall, Thomas fished out his phone and began to operate with the slightest delay. The app showed quite a number of combos, and the order may have been placed in much the same way as he had always done at home. The delivery charge was pretty much the same as usual — not more expensive because it was a service on the high-speed train. Thomas browsed through the pages excitedly before selecting two combos: one spicy beer braised duck at 37 yuan to be delivered upon arrival at Nanchang at 11:04 am and one panini at 47 yuan upon arrival at Changsha at 12:28 pm. He had placed two separate orders because he wished to experience the delivery services at different stations as scheduled. "Will the delivery boy ride to the platform on his scooter?" Thomas wondered.

As the train stopped at the Nanchang Railway Station, Thomas saw a young man carrying a white case. "My takeout must be in this case," said Thomas confidently. He waited and waited. The train was pulling out, but there was still no sign of the delivery man's scooter. Where was the takeout? Was the takeout-ordering service reliable on the high-speed train?

Restless, Thomas asked a train attendant, and the latter told him that her colleague in the dining car would deliver the takeout to the passenger's seat. Thomas felt relieved to learn this. He soon received his food, the beer braised duck combo, from the train attendant. There seemed to be nothing special with the takeout; it was soundly packed and with no leakage. Thomas opened the package, and the contents — duck meat, eggplant, and egg — were still steaming hot. He took a few mouthfuls at once and nodded his head in satisfaction.

The high-speed train arrived at Changsha, and his second takeout, the panini combo, was due. This time, Thomas was much more experienced. He was no longer anxious and waited for the delivery of his second meal at the seat. The food tasted good, too.

It took less than seven hours by high-speed train from Shanghai to Guangzhou. Here were his comments on this takeout ordering experience, "The takeout service on the high-speed train is very good. We now have a wider choice of food rather than the combo provided by the dining car and may have takeout delivered to our seats." The whole process is convenient and brings him good experience.

In recent years, the internet technology in China has been changing with each passing day, and the high-speed rail in China is developing at a high speed. Combining the two makes it possible for high-speed rail to order the takeout food. Starting July 17, 2017, passengers can order their favorite take-away meals on the high-speed rail. In 2020, 94.7% of China's cities with a population of more than one million were covered by high-speed rail networks, which include not only the Yangtze River Delta, Pearl River Delta, Bohai Rim, and other economically developed areas but also the western regions such as the Sichuan Basin, the Yunnan-Guizhou Plateau, Gansu, and Xinjiang. By the end of December 2021, the running mileage of high-speed rail in China exceeded 40,000 kilometers, ranking first in the world. The speed of high-speed rail in China provides convenience and more choices for people to travel.

生词表

生词

1. 便捷	biànjié	convenient
2. 浏览	liúlǎn	to browse
3. 抵达	dǐdá	to arrive
4. 短暂	duǎnzàn	of short duration
5. 如期	rúqī	as planned
6. 启动	qǐdòng	to start
7. 靠谱	kàopǔ	reliable
8. 情急	qíngjí	feel anxious
9. 询问	xúnwèn	ask about
10. 区别	qūbié	to distinguish
11. 渗漏	shènlòu	to seep
12. 老练	lǎoliàn	experienced
13. 焦急	jiāojí	anxious, worried
14. 覆盖	fùgài	to cover

成语、俗语、惯用语等

1. 众所周知	zhòngsuǒzhōuzhī	as everyone knows
2. 日新月异	rìxīn-yuèyì	change rapidly
3. 热气腾腾	rèqì-téngténg	steaming hot

语法点

1. 一……就……：连接一个复句，表示一个动作接着前一个动作发生或者做完一个动作以后马上开始下一个动作。

例句：他一到候车大厅就迫不及待地用手机 APP 开始操作起来。

2. 而：连词，连接动词、形容词或词组、分句等。

例句：他不再像之前那样焦急，而是耐心地等待服务员将外卖送到他的座位上。

课文结构分析

请根据这个思维导图，用完整的句子对课文进行复述。

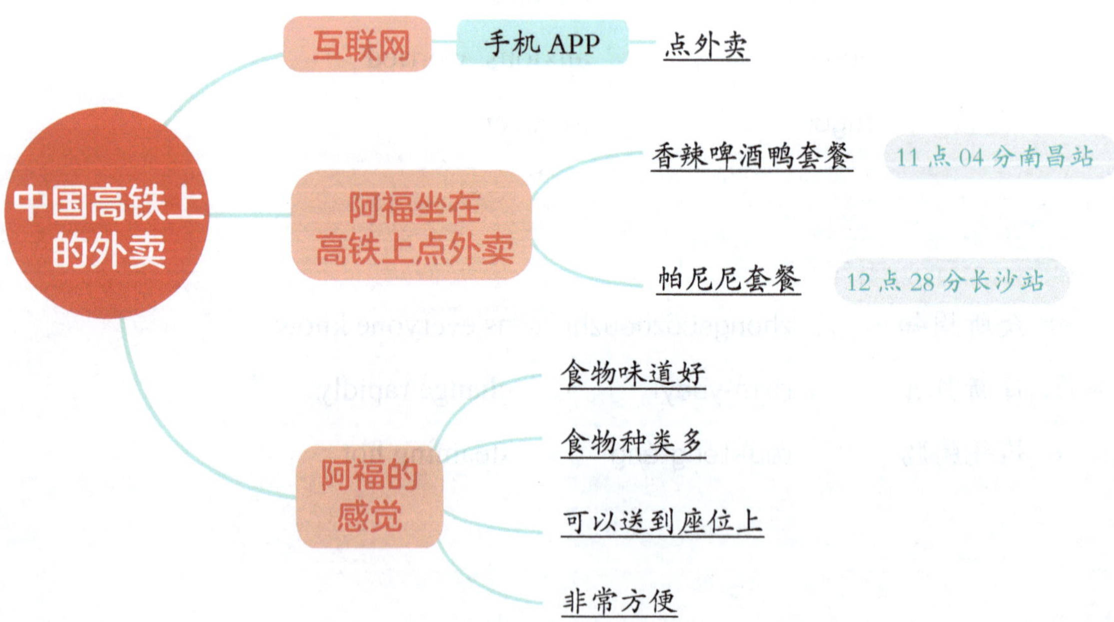

练习

1. 根据课文内容回答下面的问题。（5分）

（1）在中国如何点外卖？

（2）阿福在从哪儿到哪儿的高铁上点外卖？

（3）阿福点的第一份外卖里有什么食物？请写出两种。（2分）

（4）阿福点的第二份外卖的餐名是什么？

2. 根据课文内容完成下列表格（5分）

中国高铁发展近况

年份	发展状况	答案
什么时候？	可以在高铁上点外卖	（1）________
2020年	在100万以上人口的城市中，高铁网的覆盖率是多少？	（2）________
2021年底	高铁营运里程有多少公里？	（3）________
到2023年	高铁已达地区包括哪两个？	（4）________ （5）________

3. 从阿福的角度选择正确的答案。（5分）

（1）外卖平台上显示可点的套餐种类和数量都很多。 □

A. 正面　　B. 负面　　C. 正面和负面

（2）他等啊等，一直等到火车启动，也没看到外卖小哥来给他送餐。 □

A. 正面　　B. 负面　　C. 正面和负面

（3）外卖的包装完好，没有渗漏。 □

A. 正面　　B. 负面　　C. 正面和负面

（4）阿福在等待第二份外卖帕尼尼套餐时就显得老练多了。 □

A. 正面　　B. 负面　　C. 正面和负面

（5）在火车上点外卖感觉还是很不错的。 □

A. 正面　　B. 负面　　C. 正面和负面

课文 2　中国的共享单车

课前热身

请仔细观察下面这张图片，用两分钟左右的时间描述一下你在图片上看到了什么，以及你对图片的理解。

课文 2

扫一扫，看视频

中国的共享单车

2016 年 12 月，中国华北地区遭遇了严重的空气污染，23 个城市启动红色预警。五天的雾霾笼罩，再次唤起了人们对绿色出行的关注，也让共享单车进入了人们的视线。

自行车对于中国人来说是再熟悉不过的交通工具了。在 20 世纪六七十年代，每个家庭都梦想拥有一辆自行车。有了它，人们就觉得是过上了小康生活。到了 20 世纪八九十年代，随着生产力的发展，自行车成为大众日常生活的必备品和陪伴几代人通勤的重要交通工具。

进入到 21 世纪，中国经济繁荣发展，汽车保有量大大增加，自行车逐渐被取代，但随之而来的大城市拥堵和空气污染等问题也开始困扰城市居民。随着移动互联网的快速发展和人们环境保护意识的逐步加强，自行车以一种“共享经济”的新形态回到了中国人的视线之中。

其实，在世界上的很多国家，特别是欧洲国家，都有成熟的公共自行车租赁系统，大多由政府主导，市民通过投币或刷卡，到指定停车位租用和停靠自行车。但中国的共享单车有所不同，以目前规模最大的“哈啰单车”和“美团单车”为例，人们通过智能手机就可以快速租用和归还一辆自行车，扫描车上的二维码即可解锁车辆，而且没有固定停车位，人们可以在规定区域内自由停靠，每辆单车上都装有全球定位系统追踪器，打开手机上的应用软件就可以随时查看附近可租用车辆。

可以说，中国的共享单车行业搭上了移动互联网快速发展的便车，在智能化和便利性方面都领先了一步，这也使得它在城市中获得了飞速普及和发展。从 2015 年起，中国的共享单车数量就已经超过了其他国家的总和。

虽然共享单车的发展也经历了不少起伏，有的品牌已经退出了这一市场领域，但可以肯定的是，共享单车的出现带动了自行车相关产业的再度兴起。更为重要的是，它正在改变人们的出行观念，令人们的短距离出行变得更加方便。

China's Sharing Bike

In December 2016, North China suffered from serious air pollution, and 23 cities issued a red alert. The smog, which lasted for five days, has aroused people's concern about green travel again and brought bike-sharing into people's sight.

The bicycle is a common means of transportation for Chinese people. In the 1960s and 1970s, every family dreamed of having a bicycle which represented that the family had a well-off life. In the 1980s and 1990s, with the development of productive forces, bicycles became necessary for people's daily lives and an important vehicle for generations to commute.

Since the turn of the 21st century, China's economy has boomed, car ownership has significantly increased, and bicycles have gradually been replaced. However, the following problems, such as urban congestion and air pollution have begun to trouble urban residents. With the rapid development of the mobile net and the awakening of people's awareness of environmental protection, bicycles, in the new form of the "sharing economy", have returned to Chinese people's life.

In fact, many countries in the world, especially European countries, have their public bicycle rental systems, led mainly by the government. Citizens can rent and park bicycles at designated parking spaces by putting in coins or swiping their cards. But China's bike-sharing is different. Taking "Hellobike" and "Meituan Bike", the two largest bike rental companies at present, as examples, people can quickly rent and return a bike through their smartphones by scanning a QR code on the bike. No fixed parking space exists, and people can park freely within the specified area. Each bike is equipped with a GPS tracker, and users can check nearby available bicycles at any time by opening the application software on their mobile phones.

It can be said that the bike-sharing industry in China has taken advantage of the rapid development of mobile internet and has taken a leading step in intelligence and convenience, which has enabled it to gain rapid popularity and development in cities. Since 2015, the number of shared bicycles in China has exceeded that in other countries.

Although there have been many ups and downs in the development of the bike-sharing industry, and some brands have withdrawn from this market, the bike-sharing system has certainly driven the re-emergence of bicycle-related industries. More importantly, it is changing the choice of means of transportation for people and making short-distance travel more convenient.

生词表

生词

1. 遭遇	zāoyù	to encounter
2. 预警	yùjǐng	early warning
3. 雾霾	wùmái	smog
4. 视线	shìxiàn	line of sight
5. 通勤	tōngqín	commute
6. 繁荣	fánróng	prosperous
7. 保有量	bǎoyǒuliàng	the number of possession
8. 拥堵	yōngdǔ	traffic congestion
9. 污染	wūrǎn	to pollute
10. 困扰	kùnrǎo	to perplex
11. 共享经济	gòngxiǎng jīngjì	sharing economy
12. 租赁	zūlìn	to rent
13. 主导	zhǔdǎo	leading
14. 解锁	jiěsuǒ	to unlock
15. 全球定位系统	quánqiú dìngwèi xìtǒng	GPS
16. 追踪	zhuīzōng	to track

17. 智能化	zhìnénghuà	to intelligentialize
18. 起伏	qǐfú	rise and fall
19. 领域	lǐngyù	territory, field

成语、俗语、惯用语等

随之而来	suí zhī ér lái	happen along with

语法点

1. 对于……来说：表示从某人或某事的角度来看一件事。

例句：自行车对于中国人来说是再熟悉不过的交通工具了。

2. 随着：表示主句发生的前提条件。

例句：随着生产力的发展，自行车成为了大众日常生活的必备品和陪伴几代人通勤的重要交通工具。

3. 虽然……但……：表示转折关系的关联词。

例句：虽然共享单车的发展也经历了不少起伏，但可以肯定的是，共享单车的出现带动了自行车相关产业的再度兴起。

课文结构分析

请根据这个思维导图，用完整的句子对课文进行复述。

- 中国的共享单车
  - 20 世纪六七十年代
    - 梦想拥有一辆自行车
    - 自行车是小康生活的象征
  - 20 世纪八九十年代
    - 日常生活的必备品
    - 通勤的重要交通工具
  - 21 世纪
    - 汽车代替了自行车
    - 环境问题
      - 道路拥堵
      - 空气污染
      - 共享单车出现了
  - 共享单车
    - 移动互联网的快速发展
    - 人们环保意识的加强
  - 共享单车的使用
    - 用手机扫描车上的二维码解锁车辆
    - 没有固定停车位，方便停靠
    - 装有全球定位系统追踪器
    - 打开手机上的应用软件就可以找到可租用的单车

练习

1. 根据课文内容，把左边的解释和右边的词语对应起来。（5 分）

（1）特别了解 ☐
（2）非常重视 ☐
（3）对未来的一种期望 ☐
（4）上下班 ☐
（5）一定要有的东西 ☐

A. 关注
B. 通勤
C. 快速
D. 梦想
E. 再度
F. 熟悉
G. 取代
H. 必备品

2. 根据课文内容回答下面的问题。（5 分）

（1）20 世纪六七十年代，拥有自行车对中国家庭来说有什么象征意义？
（2）在中国，租用共享单车时，人们需要使用什么设备？
（3）人们可以把共享单车停放在哪里？
（4）人们怎样才可以找到共享单车？为什么？（2 分）

3. 根据课文内容判断下列说法的对错，并说明理由。（5 分）

	对	错
（1）严重的空气污染使得绿色出行受到了人们的关注。	☐	☐
理由：____________________		
（2）21 世纪，中国家庭把自行车当作出行的主要交通工具。	☐	☐
理由：____________________		
（3）中国只有两家共享单车公司。	☐	☐
理由：____________________		
（4）中国的共享单车数量和一个欧洲国家的差不多。	☐	☐
理由：____________________		
（5）共享单车令人们可以更加方便地去到不太远的地方。	☐	☐
理由：____________________		

拓展练习

话题活动

活动 A

观看中国中央电视台的系列纪录片《中国高铁》（共 3 集），直观地了解中国高铁的建设和运营情况，理解高铁对中国人出行的意义。

活动 B

观看中国中央电视台的系列纪录片《共享经济》（共 2 集），了解“交换代替购买，共用代替占有”的新生活方式，思考“共享经济现如今处于初级阶段，但在未来它会发展成一个新的商业模式，这是一个新兴市场”这个话题。

话题讨论

看完以上关于共享经济的纪录片，请以“互联网时代下的共享经济”为主题进行小组讨论。内容包括：共享经济的种类；共享经济的平台有哪些；共享经济对日常生活的影响；共享经济对商业的影响；共享经济与环保的关系；你希望还可以共享什么；共享经济的前景。

写作练习

你和好朋友在刚过去的假期去中国的大城市游玩了一周。结合“读万卷书不如行万里路”这句话的意思，写一篇 500 ~ 700 字的博客文章，介绍你们这次旅游的经历，特别是你观察到的当地人的出行方式，以及你的看法。

文化点

中国磁悬浮列车

中国磁悬浮列车是指中国开发和应用的磁悬浮交通系统。磁悬浮列车利用磁力原理悬浮在轨道上，并通过磁力驱动系统来推进列车运行。中国是世界上最早实现磁悬浮列车商业运营的国家，已拥有两条线路。

目前，中国最著名的磁悬浮列车线路是上海磁悬浮列车。上海磁悬浮列车于2002年开始商业运营，连接上海市区和浦东国际机场。它是世界上商业运营最长的磁悬浮线路，全长30.5公里。上海磁悬浮列车采用了高温超导磁悬浮技术，列车可以以最高时速约431公里运行，提供快速、高效的城市机场连接。此外，中国还在其他城市进行了磁悬浮列车的试验和建设，例如，长沙磁悬浮快线是中国首条商业运营的中低速磁悬浮线路，连接了长沙市区和黄花国际机场。

磁悬浮列车在提高交通速度、减少能源消耗和环境污染方面具有潜力，对未来城市交通的发展具有重要意义。

话题五 节庆

教学内容和目标	文化点
1. 了解中国人庆祝传统节日的习俗和文化含义。 2. 了解中国少数民族节日的习俗和文化含义。	中秋节，月饼，赏月，泼水节，新年俗

课文 1　月饼——中国人亲情的纽带

课前热身

请仔细观察下面这张图片，用两分钟左右的时间描述一下你在图片上看到了什么，以及你对图片的理解。

课文 1

扫一扫，看视频

月饼——中国人亲情的纽带

每年农历八月十五是中国的传统节日——中秋节。在这一天，中国人会赏明月、吃月饼、看花灯。中国有句俗话：民以食为天。传统节日中的特色饮食将中国的文化精髓发挥得淋漓尽致，比如春节吃饺子、元宵节吃汤圆、端午节吃粽子，而月饼这道美食也成为中秋节的文化符号。

中秋节最早体现的是古代中国人对月亮的崇拜。在中国古代，皇帝有春天祭日、秋天祭月的习俗。农历八月十五当天，月亮会形成又圆又亮的满月，而这一天恰好在秋季的中间，所以称为“中秋”。从唐代开始，中秋节成为中国固定的传统节日，一代代传承下来。

月饼本是中秋节时用来祭奉月神的祭品，最初称为“胡饼”。月饼这个名字的由来，相传跟中国古代四大美女之一的杨贵妃有关。传说有一年中秋，唐玄宗和杨贵妃赏月吃胡饼时，杨贵妃仰望皎洁的明月，被美景感染，于是给胡饼改名为“月饼”。后来，祭月习俗传入平常百姓家。每当中秋之夜月亮升起，全家人围桌而坐，分食月饼，共享天伦之乐。如果家中有人未归，也要留下一角月饼，以示全家团圆。“但愿人长久，千里共婵娟”，中国宋代词人苏轼的这句诗表现了人们在中秋节里对团圆的渴望。因此，中秋节又被视为“团圆节”，月饼也成为团圆的象征。

中国的月饼种类繁多，按产地分有苏式、广式、京式等，就口味而言，有甜的也有咸的。月饼除了有代表团圆的传统圆形之外，还有正方、八角、三角等形状。其馅料则有冰糖、豆沙、五仁、枣泥、火腿、蛋黄等数十种。如今，随着时代的发展，市场上还出现了冰淇淋、巧克力、水果等新奇口味。除了中国品牌，一些国外品牌也推出了独具特色的月饼。月饼正逐渐走向海外市场，成为受人们欢迎的节日食品。

每一个节日都是民族文化长期沉淀的结果。虽然月饼的样式和口味不断推陈出新，但是其内涵始终不变。圆圆的月饼不仅寄托着中国人浓浓的亲情和乡情，更传承着淳朴而深远的中国文化。

Mooncake —A Snack for Family Reunion

The Mid-Autumn Festival falls on the 15th day of the eighth month of China's lunar calendar. Chinese people celebrate this holiday by enjoying the full moon, the lanterns and eating mooncakes. As a Chinese saying goes, "Food is the prime need." The special food Chinese people make on traditional holidays is a perfect example. They make dumplings during the Spring Festival, sweet dumplings made of glutinous rice flour during the Lantern Festival, and pyramid-shaped dumplings made of glutinous rice wrapped in bamboo or reed leaves for the Dragon Boat Festival. Mooncakes are the delicacy representative of the Mid-Autumn Festival.

During the Mid-Autumn Festival, people follow the ancient Chinese custom of worshipping the moon. Emperors in ancient China are said to have obeyed the ritual of offering sacrifices to the sun in the spring and to the moon in the autumn. The moon is full and splendid on the 15th day of the eighth month of the Chinese lunar calendar. This day marks the middle of the autumn season, and it is thus called "mid-autumn". The day has been a holiday since the Tang Dynasty (618-907) and handed down to the later generations.

Mooncakes were once used as offerings to the goddess of the moon during the Mid-Autumn Festival. It used to be called "hubing". Legend has it that on one Mid-Autumn Festival, Emperor Xuanzong of the Tang Dynasty and his favorite consort Yang Yuhuan were enjoying the moon and eating "hubing" when she was deeply attracted by the splendor of the moon that she decided to call it a "yuebing (mooncake)". Later, ordinary Chinese people started to worship and enjoy the moon from that day. When the moon rises during the Mid-Autumn Festival, all family members sit around the table, eating mooncakes and enjoying family happiness together. If any family members are absent, they hold onto a piece of the cake for them to symbolize a family reunion. Su Shi, a famous poet of the Song Dynasty (960-1279), wrote, "May we all be blessed with longevity. Though thousands of miles apart, we share the beauty of the moon together." This expressed the people's wishes for reunion with their families during the Mid-Autumn Festival. This is why the festival is also called the Reunion Festival and why the mooncake symbolizes family reunion.

There are a variety of mooncakes in China. They can be classified according to different places. For example, there are Suzhou, Cantonese, and Beijing mooncakes. They differ in taste, sweet or salty. The shapes of mooncakes also differ. Apart from traditional round mooncakes, which symbolize reunion, there are also square, octagonal, and triangular ones. The most common stuffing of the mooncakes are rock candy, sweet bean paste, and five nuts (typically including walnuts, pumpkin seeds, watermelon seeds, peanuts, and sesame seeds). Some other popular stuffing include jujube paste, ham, egg yolk, and other things. Over time, ingredients such as ice cream, chocolate, and fruits have been added, giving a modern flavors to the ancient mooncake. In addition to Chinese mooncakes, some special mooncakes are produced by foreign companies. Mooncakes are expanding into the markets overseas and gaining popularity abroad.

Holidays embody the culture of a nation. Although the shapes and tastes of mooncakes are always changing, their meaning remains unchanged. Mooncakes represent the Chinese people's love for their families and hometowns while passing on the deep roots of traditional Chinese culture.

生词表

生词

1. 特色饮食	tèsè yǐnshí	special cuisine
2. 精髓	jīngsuǐ	essence
3. 符号	fúhào	symbol
4. 崇拜	chóngbài	to worship
5. 祭品	jìpǐn	sacrifice
6. 皎洁	jiǎojié	bright and clear
7. 感染	gǎnrǎn	to infect
8. 繁多	fánduō	various
9. 沉淀	chéndiàn	to deposit
10. 内涵	nèihán	connotation
11. 寄托	jìtuō	place on
12. 淳朴	chúnpǔ	simple

成语、俗语、惯用语等

1. 淋漓尽致	línlí-jìnzhì	thoroughly
2. 天伦之乐	tiānlúnzhīlè	enjoy family happiness together
3. 但愿人长久，千里共婵娟	dànyuàn rén chángjiǔ, qiānlǐ gòng chánjuān	May we live long and share the beauty of the moon together, even if we are hundreds of miles apart.
4. 推陈出新	tuīchén-chūxīn	weed through the old to bring forth the new

语法点

就……而言：可用于限制评论的范围。

例句：就口味而言，有甜的也有咸的。

课文结构分析

请根据这个思维导图，用完整的句子对课文进行复述。

- 月饼
  - 中秋节
    - 农历八月十五
    - 中国的传统节日
    - 团圆节
  - 中秋节节庆活动
    - 赏明月
      - 又圆又亮的满月
    - 吃月饼
      - 种类繁多
        - 产地：苏式、广式、京式
        - 口味：甜的、咸的
        - 形状：正方、八角、三角
        - 馅料：冰糖、豆沙、五仁、枣泥、火腿、蛋黄
    - 月饼原本的含义
      - 春天祭日、秋天祭月
      - 祭奉月神的祭品
  - 中秋节的意义
    - 全家团圆
    - 共享天伦之乐
    - 但愿人长久，千里共婵娟

练习

1. 根据课文内容回答下面的问题。（5 分）

（1）在古代，中秋节体现了人们对什么的崇拜？

（2）杨贵妃是谁？

（3）中秋之夜，如果有家人没有回来，其他人会怎么做？

（4）“但愿人长久，千里共婵娟”有什么含义？

（5）月饼按产地分为哪三种？

2. 根据课文内容选择正确的答案。（5 分）

（1）下面哪一件不是中国人为庆祝中秋节而做的事？ □

A. 赏明月

B. 吃月饼

C. 看花灯

D. 划龙舟

（2）中秋节最早体现的是 ________。 □

A. 皇帝对月亮的崇拜

B. 中国人对月亮的崇拜

C. 皇帝春天祭月的习惯

D. 杨贵妃对月亮的喜爱

（3）中秋节是从什么时候成为中国固定的传统节日的？ □

A. 唐朝

B. 宋代

C. 清朝

D. 民国

（4）月饼最初是做什么用的？ □

A. 祭奉日神

B. 祭奉月神

C. 美食

D. 点心

（5）月饼是什么的象征？ □

A. 开心

B. 健康

C. 团圆

D. 浪漫

3. 根据课文内容判断下面说法的对错，并说明理由。（5分）

	对	错
（1）中秋节那天的月亮特别圆也特别亮。	□	□
理由：________________		
（2）月饼的口味不只有甜的。	□	□
理由：________________		
（3）月饼的形状只有圆形。	□	□
理由：________________		
（4）月饼只在中国受欢迎。	□	□
理由：________________		
（5）随着时间的推移，月饼的内涵不断在变。	□	□
理由：________________		

4. 上网找出有关中国传统节日的信息，完成下面的表格。

中国传统节日

中国传统节日	**时间**	**节庆活动**	**节庆代表食品**
春节	农历 月 日	拜年、送红包、贴对联、吃团圆饭	饺子、年糕、鱼
元宵节			
清明节			
端午节			
中秋节			

课文2　泼水节

课前热身

请仔细观察下面这张图片，用两分钟左右的时间描述一下你在图片上看到了什么，以及你对图片的理解。

课文 2

扫一扫，看视频

泼水节

在傣族人看来，水是圣洁、美好、光明的象征。每逢一年一度的泼水节，人们走出大街小巷，追逐嬉戏，用各种各样的容器盛水互相泼洒，象征着吉祥的一朵朵水花在空中盛开。人们尽情地欢呼，全身湿透，笑声朗朗，欢快热闹。

傣族泼水节又名“浴佛节”，是傣族的“新年”。泼水节一般在傣历每年的六月中旬，也就是公历 4 月中旬左右举行。2006 年 5 月 20 日，中国云南省西双版纳傣族自治州申报的傣族泼水节被列入第一批国家级非物质文化遗产名录。

泼水节起源于傣族的一个古老神话故事。相传，在遥远的过去，有一位名叫尼洛的神女，她能够使用水的力量治愈疾病和驱赶邪恶。为了感谢尼洛的神力，傣族人在每年的 4 月举行泼水节向尼洛祈福，用水洗掉过去一年的不顺，让水为新的一年带来好运与祝福。随着时间的推移，泼水节逐渐成为傣族的重要传统节日，并在云南地区其他民族中也得到了传承和发展。

每年泼水节来临之际，傣家人便忙着杀猪、杀鸡、酿酒，用糯米做成各种美味的食品，在节日里享用。

大规模的节庆活动主要安排在泼水节的第三天。傣族人能歌善舞，泼水节自然少不了舞蹈，象脚舞和孔雀舞就是他们喜爱的舞蹈。从七八岁的娃娃到七八十岁的老人都会穿上节日盛装聚集到广场上，参加集体舞蹈。

赛龙舟是泼水节最精彩的项目之一。人们欢聚在澜沧江畔、瑞丽江边，观看龙舟大赛。比赛一开始，整装待发的龙舟便像箭一般往前飞去，节日的欢乐气氛在此时达到了高潮。除了龙舟大赛以外，“放高升”和“孔明灯”也是泼水节期间特有的活动。高升是傣族人自制的一种烟火。人们在节前就搭好高射架，届时将自制的烟花点燃，烟花在空中绚丽绽放，光彩夺目。孔明灯是一种可以利用热气球原理升空的纸制灯笼。入夜，人们在广场空地上将灯烛点燃，把一盏盏“孔明灯”放飞上天，以此许下愿望，希望新的一年风调雨顺，幸福美满。

对于傣族的未婚青年男女来说，泼水节更是他们寻觅爱情的美好时节。在泼水节期间，他们会玩儿一种“丢包”游戏：姑娘把用花布精心制作的花包当作爱情的信物，花包在姑娘和小伙儿们的手中飞来飞去，情投意合的男女就会双双悄悄退出丢包场地，单独进行交流。

泼水节是全面展现傣族水文化、音乐舞蹈文化、饮食文化、服饰文化等传统文化的综合舞台，是研究傣族历史的重要窗口。同时，泼水节还是加强西双版纳全州各族人民团结的重要纽带，在促进西双版纳与东南亚各国友好合作交流方面也起到了积极作用。

Water-Splashing Festival

For the Dai ethnic group, water is a symbol of holiness, pleasure, and light. During the annual Water-Splashing Festival, people flock to the streets with pots, bottles, buckets and so on, where they uninhibitedly Splashing and spray each other with water to wish a happy new year and good fortune. Although they get wet, they are cheerful and full of laughter.

The Water-Splashing Festival, also called "Bathing the Buddha Festival", marks the Dai New Year. Based on the Dai calendar, the Dai New Year generally falls around the middle of the sixth month (mid-April of the Gregorian calendar). On May 20, 2006, the Dai Water-Splashing Festival, submitted by the Xishuangbanna Dai Autonomous Prefecture, was among the first to be included in the national list of Intangible Cultural Heritage in China.

The Water-Splashing Festival originated from an ancient myth of the Dai people. Legend has it that in the distant past, a goddess named Niluo could use water to cure diseases and drive away evil. To thank Niluo's divine power, the Dai people hold a water-Splashinging festival every April to pray for Niluo to wash away the past year's troubles with water and bring good luck and blessings to the new year. Over time, the Water-Splashing Festival has gradually become an important traditional festival of the Dai people, and it has also been inherited and developed by other ethnic groups in Yunnan.

As the Water-Splashing Festival nears, the Dai people will lose no time making various preparations, from slaughtering livestock and brewing wine to making rice cakes and snacks.

The climax of the festival is on the third day of the Water-Splashing Festival. The Dai people are naturally good singers and dancers, and dancing is indispensable to the festival celebrations. The typical dances of the Dai people include the Elephant Feet Dance and the Peacock Dance. Everyone in the local communities, from 7-year-old kids to seniors in their 70s and 80s, will wear traditional clothes and gather at the central squares of local villages to dance together.

Dragon boat racing is another spectacular activity held during the Water-Splashing Festival. Local people gather at the banks of the Lancang River or Ruili River to watch dragon boat races. The dragon boats are held still until the signal is given. They abruptly set off like arrows, marking the culmination of the Water-Splashing Festival. "Home-made fireworks" and "Kongming Lanterns" are also popular during the festival. Local people prepare the launcher before the festival, and at the festival, they light up "home-made fireworks" which burst into brillant and dazzling flames. At night, they light up and fly "Kongming Lanterns" (paper lamps that use the principle of hot air balloons to lift off) at public squares to pray for good weather and happiness in the new year.

The Water-Splashing Festival is also an occasion for Dai youths to look for their loved ones. A game called "Dropping Bags" is very popular among them. Girls make delicate "flower bags" with a fine cloth as a token of love, which is then thrown between girls and boys. When a girl and a boy feel they have found a good match, they will exit the game to communicate privately.

The Water-Splashing Festival presents a fantastic stage to show the Dai culture, especially their water culture, music, dancing, cuisine, costumes, and folk culture. It also provides an important platform to catch a glimpse of Dai history. Meanwhile, the Water-Splashing Festival helps strengthen the bonds and feelings of unity among the various ethnic groups in Xishuangbanna Dai Autonomous Prefecture. It also positively contributes to their friendly cooperation and exchanges with neighboring Southeast Asian countries.

生词表

生词

1. 容器	róngqì	container
2. 嬉戏	xīxì	to play
3. 尽情	jìnqíng	to one's heart's content
4. 遥远	yáoyuǎn	remote
5. 治愈	zhìyù	to cure
6. 驱赶	qūgǎn	to drive
7. 邪恶	xié'è	evil, vicious
8. 酿酒	niàng jiǔ	make wine
9. 糯米	nuòmǐ	glutinous rice
10. 绚丽	xuànlì	gorgeous

成语、俗语、惯用语等

1. 大街小巷	dàjiē-xiǎoxiàng	streets and lanes
2. 整装待发	zhěngzhuāng-dàifā	get ready for a journey or a march
3. 光彩夺目	guāngcǎi-duómù	splendid
4. 风调雨顺	fēngtiáo-yǔshùn	favorable weather

语法点

像……一般：比喻句。

例句：比赛一开始，整装待发的龙舟便像箭一般往前飞去。

课文结构分析

请根据这个思维导图，用完整的句子对课文进行复述。

- 泼水节
  - 传统节日
    - 又称“浴佛节”
    - 傣族的“新年”
    - 国家级非物质文化遗产
  - 时间
    - 傣历6月中旬
    - 公历4月中旬
  - 由来
    - 神话故事
    - 尼洛用水治病和驱邪
  - 节庆活动
    - 节前
      - 杀猪、杀鸡、酿酒
      - 用糯米做美食
    - 节日期间
      - 三天庆祝活动
      - 泼水
      - 唱歌跳舞
      - 赛龙舟
      - “放高升”和“孔明灯”
  - 意义
    - 用水洗掉过去一年的不顺
    - 为新的一年带来好运与祝福

练习

1. 根据课文内容，从右边选出最合适的结尾来完成左边的短句。（5 分）

（1）人们用各种各样的容器盛水 □

（2）泼水节起源于 □

（3）泼水节逐渐成为 □

（4）象脚舞和孔雀舞 □

（5）整装待发的龙舟 □

A. 流传下来。
B. 互祝平安幸福。
C. 像箭一般往前飞去。
D. 一个神话故事。
E. 互相泼洒。
F. 傣族的重要传统节日。
G. 是他们喜爱的舞蹈。
H. 达到了高潮。

2. 用课文中的词语填空。（5 分）

（1）每逢 ________ 的春节，家家户户都点上各式各样的彩灯，热闹极了。

（2）在妈妈生日那天，我向她送上我的________。

（3）在同学的帮助下，我的成绩________变好了。

（4）小明不仅________，而且学习成绩也特别优秀。

（5）马上就要毕业了，我为老师________了一张感谢卡。

3. 根据课文内容回答下面的问题。（5 分）

（1）为什么说傣族泼水节对未婚青年有特别的意义？（1 分）

（2）为什么说傣族泼水节是研究傣族历史的重要窗口？（4 分）

拓展练习

话题活动

1. 观看微电影《中秋节》，了解为什么中秋节也叫“团圆节”。
2. 做一个海报，介绍你自己国家最重要的传统节日。

话题讨论

随着人类步入信息化社会，中西方文化也在互相渗透，相互融合，中西方传统节日的全球化特征越来越明显。面对这种情况，有人支持也有人抵制。分组进行辩论，正方的观点：中西方传统节日文化的融合对于本土文化来说利大于弊。反方的观点：中西方传统节日文化的融合对于本土文化来说弊大于利。你同意哪种观点？用 500~700 字阐述你的观点，要求观点明确，有理有据。

写作练习

你的学校将组织一次多元文化周活动，你要做一次演讲，题目是“传承本国传统文化的重要性”。请用 500 ～ 700 字写一篇演讲稿，题目自拟。

文化点

中国人新的过年习俗

新的过年习俗，简称新年俗，指的是不同于中国新年（春节）传统习俗的现代化和个性化的过年习俗。

送祝福，人们会通过短信、电话、社交媒体等方式向亲朋好友发送新年祝福，表达对他们的关心和祝福。

旅游，越来越多的人选择在春节假期出游，探索国内外的旅游景点。这也是人们享受假期、放松心情的方式之一。

线上发红包，随着移动支付的普及，现在许多人选择通过手机红包的形式给亲友发送祝福和礼金。通过手机应用程序，人们可以发送和接收电子红包，增加了方便性和趣味性。

这些习俗反映了中国社会的变化和现代化的影响。它们既延续了传统的习俗和价值观，又融入了当代的生活方式和娱乐方式，为人们带来了更多的选择和乐趣。

话题六 消费

教学内容和目标	文化点
1. 了解中国人购物的主要方式和特点。 2. 理解中国人购物方式的多样性。	网购，直播，夜市，移动支付，购物节

大角咀廟會
Tai Kok Tsui Temple
街市
歡迎光臨

课文1　祝您用餐愉快

课前热身

请仔细观察下面这张图片，用两分钟左右的时间描述一下你在图片上看到了什么，以及你对图片的理解。

课文 1

扫一扫，看视频

祝您用餐愉快

“中国的外卖服务实在太神奇了，只要手机上下单，外卖小哥在半小时之内就能将外卖送到我们手上，这个速度实在令人惊叹。”为了更好地了解外卖这个行业，亲身体验中国外卖小哥一天的生活，来自北京大学的外国留学生小高在外卖平台申请成为一名外卖小哥，审核通过之后，他就正式接单了。

由于一开始不熟悉软件的运用和接单的流程，小高有些手忙脚乱。再加上第一单路途较远，他迟到了整整半个小时才将外卖送到顾客手中。虽然顾客并没有给差评，但看都不看他一眼，也没有说声感谢，冷漠地接过外卖并关上了大门。这让小高感到十分懊恼和挫败。

送了几单之后，小高渐渐找到了感觉，他甚至开始学习其他外卖小哥，尝试一次接多个订单。手机上接单，去店铺拿外卖，规划出最省时的路线，最终把外卖送到顾客们的手上。“祝您用餐愉快！”每一次把外卖送到，小高都会愉快地向顾客送出祝福。每遇到一个对他的服务表示满意的顾客，他都觉得特别开心。体验之后，小高感慨地说：“送外卖一点儿都不容易。它需要很高的智商、很强的学习能力和快速反应的能力。外卖员经常同时收到很多个单子，他们需要做出非常快速的决定，配合外卖平台的后台系统，安排好最省时的取外卖和送外卖的路线，这样才能在最短的时间内将外卖送到顾客手中。”

傍晚时分是外卖订单的晚高峰时期，小高开始接到源源不断的订单。这时候的他也已经得心应手了许多。

这一整天外卖小哥的工作，小高从上午10点忙到晚上10点才完成了17单，总共赚到了80块人民币。而在北京，外卖“单王”每天的送单数是84单，其他的外卖员每人每天接单平均在40单以上，每月能拿到的工资平均为6500～8000元人民币。在结束工作回家的路上，小高看到还有很多外卖小哥仍在寒风中站着，等着送宵夜。他不禁感慨道：“今天我才发现，其实中国人才是全世界最拼最努力的民族。”

通过这次特别的体验，小高非常佩服中国人吃苦耐劳的品质。他说：“怪不得只有在中国这片土地上，外卖这样的行业才能蓬勃发展。”中国人努力工作、追求效率、对工作认真负责的精神让小高深刻地认识到，中国高速发展的背后是这些普通中国人在为此不懈努力着。

Enjoy Your Meal

Xiao Gao is an international student at Peking University. “The food delivery service industry in China is amazing. Delivery drivers can deliver food in half an hour. This speed is really amazing.” To better understand this industry and gain first-hand experience as a delivery driver in China, Xiao Gao applied for the job. After passing the application check, he began to work.

At first, being not familiar with the software and the process of receiving orders, he was a little in a rush. His first order was far away, and he was half an hour late. The customer didn't give him a negative review but coldly took the delivery and indifferently closed the door without looking at him or thanking him. This made Xiao Gao feel very upset and frustrated.

After finishing a few more orders, he gradually got the hang of it and even learned how to receive multiple orders at a time and ake the most saving time route to deliver the orders like other delivery drivers. "Enjoy your meal," he said, happily delivering his good wishes to a customer. When a customer was satisfied with his delivery service, he felt very pleased. While waiting for more orders, he emotionally said, "So far, I am keenly aware that the takeout delivery is not easy at all. It requires a high IQ and a strong ability to learn and respond quickly. Delivery drivers often receive many orders at the same time, and they need to make quick decisions to arrange the routes to pick up and deliver the food to customers in the shortest time."

At dusk, all the delivery drivers were very busy receiving orders during peak hours, as was Xiao Gao. By this time, however, he could handle the orders much better.

On his first day, Xiao Gao worked from 10 am to 10 pm, finished 17 orders, and earned a total of 80 yuan. In Beijing, the record number of daily orders completed by a delivery driver is 84. Many delivery drivers receive more than 40 orders daily, and their average monthly salary is 6,500-8,500 yuan. On the way home after work, Xiao Gao saw many delivery drivers still standing in the cold wind, waiting to deliver midnight snacks. He says emotionally, "Today I realized that Chinese people are the most hardworking in the world."

Through this special experience, Xiao Gao was deeply impressed by the hardworking spirit of the Chinese people. "It is no wonder that only in China can such an industry thrive," he said. By seeing the hard work of the Chinese people, as well as their efficiency, conscientiousness, and responsible attitude, Xiao Gao realized that China's rapid development cannot be separated from the unremitting efforts of these ordinary Chinese people.

生词表

生词

1. 审核	shěnhé	examine and verify
2. 流程	liúchéng	process
3. 冷漠	lěngmò	unconcerned
4. 懊恼	àonǎo	be annoyed
5. 挫败	cuòbài	to frustrate
6. 规划	guīhuà	planning
7. 感慨	gǎnkǎi	sigh with emotion
8. 晚高峰	wǎn gāofēng	evening rush hour
9. 源源不断	yuányuán-búduàn	a steady flow of
10. 宵夜	xiāoyè	night snack
11. 蓬勃	péngbó	vigorous
12. 不懈	búxiè	untiring

成语、俗语、惯用语等

1. 手忙脚乱	shǒumáng-jiǎoluàn	be in a rush
2. 得心应手	déxīn-yìngshǒu	work with high proficiency
3. 吃苦耐劳	chīkǔ-nàiláo	endure hardships and stand hard work

语法点

怪不得：表示明白了原因，对发生的某种事情就不觉得奇怪。

例句：怪不得只有在中国这片土地上，外卖这样的行业才能蓬勃发展。

课文结构分析

请根据这个思维导图，用完整的句子对课文进行复述。

- 祝您用餐愉快
  - 小高
    - 北京大学的外国留学生
    - ______
  - 时间
    - 从上午10点到晚上10点
    - 完成了17单
    - 总收入80块人民币
  - 对外卖工作的看法
    - 不容易
    - 很强的学习能力
    - 快速的反应能力
  - 对中国人的看法
    - 全世界最拼最努力的民族
    - 吃苦耐劳的品质
    - 努力工作、追求效率
    - 对工作认真负责

练习

1. 根据课文内容回答下面的问题。（10 分）

（1）在中国，怎样可以叫到外卖？（2 分）

（2）小高为什么要去送外卖？（2 分）

（3）小高送的第一单外卖顺利吗？为什么？（2 分）

（4）送完第一单外卖后，小高为什么感到懊恼和挫败？（3 分）

（5）根据第③段，小高对外卖小哥的工作有什么看法？请写出一个例子。（1 分）

2. 根据课文内容，把左边的词语和右边的反义词对应起来。（5 分）

（1）源源不断	□	A. 衰退溃败
		B. 断断续续
（2）得心应手	□	C. 消极懒散
		D. 束手无策
（3）吃苦耐劳	□	E. 虎头蛇尾
		F. 积极向上
（4）蓬勃发展	□	G. 好吃懒做
（5）不懈努力	□	H. 生命不止

课文2　“双十一”购物节

课前热身

请仔细观察下面这张图片，用两分钟左右的时间描述一下你在图片上看到了什么，以及你对图片的理解。

课文 2

扫一扫，看视频

“双十一”购物节

11月11日是中国最火爆的电商促销日和网络购物狂欢日。在那一天，各大电商为了增加销量绞尽脑汁，比如，2021年推出了时装秀、直播秀等“新玩法”，交易额也突破了千亿元人民币。

现在，大部分中国人，只要在家里打开电脑或手机，就可以足不出户在网上购买到需要的商品和服务。除了买衣物和生活用品之外，还可以购买水果蔬菜，也可以花钱请大厨到家里做一顿晚餐。此外，网络上还有各种你想不到的新奇物品，比如，花20块钱买一袋大山里的新鲜空气。

中国绝大部分零售商都在天猫或其他电商平台上开了网店。线上线下的充分融合，加上人们逐渐形成了网络购物的习惯，让“双十一”网购狂欢日呈现出巨大的消费能力。此外，近年来，中国物流行业的发展也为电商产业和消费市场的繁荣带来了巨大能量。

从网购品种和类别的丰富以及餐饮、文化、旅游、教育、金融等产品在网络上的活跃交易可以看出，虽然中国的传统产业增长放缓，但第三产业的活力和消费领域的多样化在不断增强。这让中国在经济增速放缓的背景下，仍然拥有强大的市场潜力。

很多经济学家认为，“双十一”不仅仅是“网购现象”，它更是中国消费能力和经济活力的体现。

Double 11, the Online Shopping Festival

Double 11 on November 11th is the biggest shopping promotion activity for online shoppers and e-commerce platforms in China. Before that day, the major Chinese e-commerce sites rack their heads for marketing campaigns. For example, in 2021, fashion shows, live-stream, and other "new ways of promotion" were launched, and the trading volume exceeded 100 billion yuan.

Nowadays, it is from habit for most Chinese people to buy products or service on the internet by using mobile phones or computers. In addition to buying clothes and other goods, they can order a chef to cook their dinner at home. Moreover, there are other strange things sold on the internet that are beyond one's imagination. For example, you can buy a bag of fresh air from the mountains for 20 RMB yuan.

Most Chinese retailers have opened stores on Tmall or other e-commerce platforms. Online and offline businesses are now fully integrated, and people's desires to shop online have grown, fueling momentum for the Double 11 online shopping festival. The development of logistics industry in China has contributed significantly to the prosperity of China's e-commerce and consumer market.

The variety of items sold online, particularly from the food and drinks, to culture, tourism, education, and finance products, demonstrates the vitality of the tertiary industry and the growing diversity of the consumer market. This amounts to great market potential despite the slower growth of tradition industries.

Moreover, many economists believe that Double 11 is more than an online shopping activity, as it embodies China's growing consumption power and economic vitality.

生词表

生词

1. 火爆	huǒbào	hot
2. 促销	cùxiāo	sales promotion
3. 狂欢	kuánghuān	revelry
4. 新奇	xīnqí	novel, strange
5. 放缓	fànghuǎn	slow down
6. 第三产业	dì-sān chǎnyè	tertiary industry
7. 领域	lǐngyù	territory

成语、俗语、惯用语等

1. 绞尽脑汁	jiǎojìn-nǎozhī	rack one's head
2. 足不出户	zúbùchūhù	stay indoors

语法点

1. 从……可以看出：一般是通过某种表象推测一种结论或者结果。

例句： 从网购品种和类别的丰富以及餐饮、文化、旅游、教育、金融等产品在网络上的活跃交易可以看出，虽然中国的传统产业增长放缓，但第三产业的活力和消费领域的多样化在不断增强。

2. 不仅仅……更是……：表示递进关系的关联词。

例句： "双十一"不仅仅是"网购现象"，它更是中国消费能力和经济活力的体现。

课文结构分析

请根据这个思维导图，用完整的句子对课文进行复述。

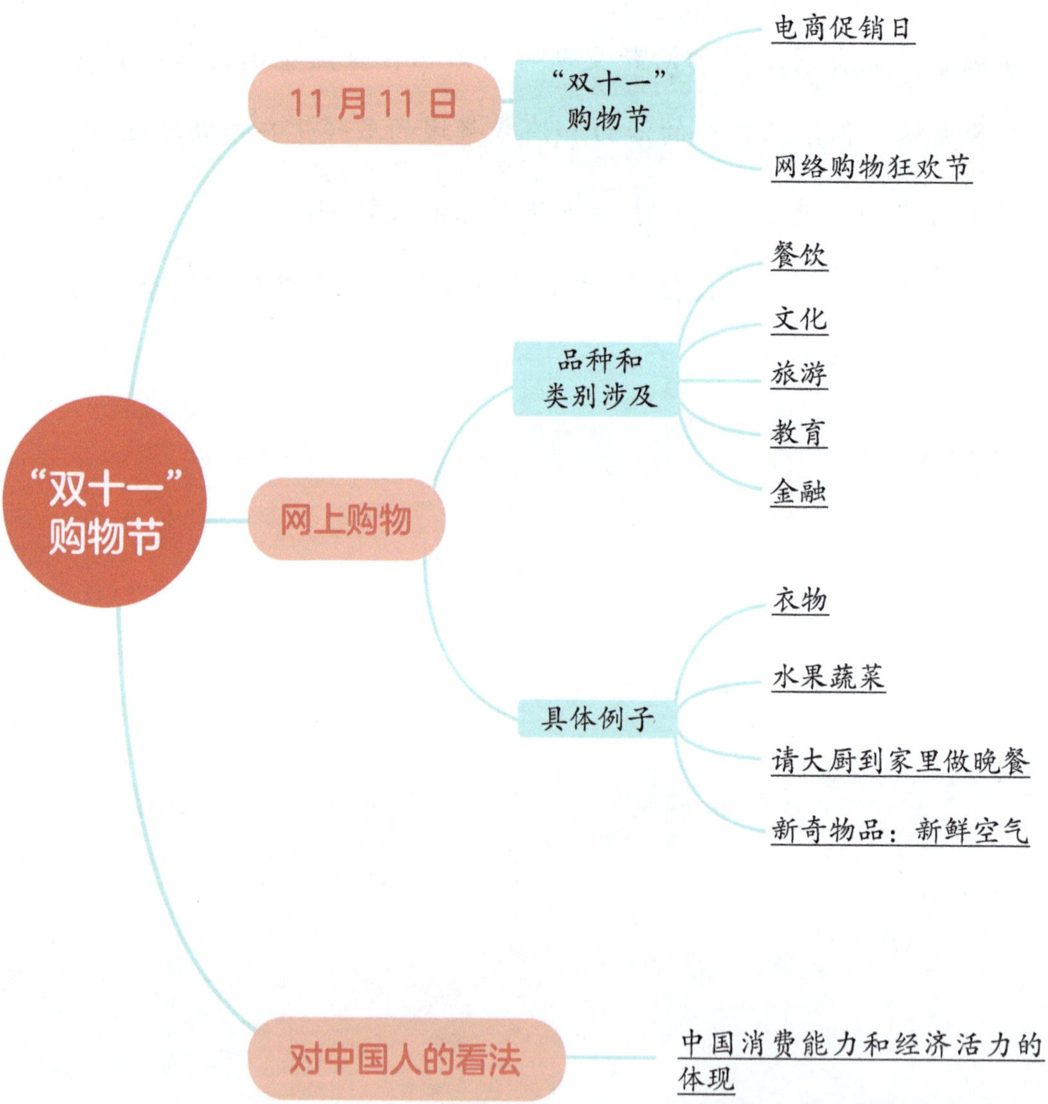

练习

1. 根据课文内容回答下面的问题。（5 分）

（1）“双十一”是一个什么样的日子？（2 分）

（2）2021 年“双十一”的交易额有多少？（1 分）

（3）在网上花 20 块可以买到什么新奇物品？（1 分）

（4）电商最为依赖的是哪个行业？请写出一个例子。（1 分）

2. 根据课文内容选择正确答案。（5 分）

（1）11 月 11 日，电商们想尽办法 ________ 。 □

A. 举办时装秀

B. 开办直播秀

C. 增加销售量

D. 免费送礼物

（2）在中国，年轻人喜欢________。 □

A. 走出家门

B. 上网购买

C. 玩电脑游戏

D. 打电话聊天

（3）如果不想自己做饭，可以________。 □

A. 去外面的超市买蔬菜水果

B. 去外面的餐厅吃

C. 上网请厨师到家里来做饭

D. 叫家人去厨房做

（4）“天猫”是________。 □

A. 电商平台

B. 时装网店

C. 物流公司

D. 快递公司

（5）“双十一”体现了__________。 □

A. 中国极强的网络速度

B. 中国的传统产业增长

C. 中国的完善的快递业

D. 中国的经济活力

3. 根据课文内容判断下列说法的对错，并说明理由。（5 分）

	对	错
（1）“双十一”是中国最受欢迎的网购日。	□	□
理由：________________________________		
（2）网上购物只包括衣物和生活用品。	□	□
理由：________________________________		
（3）现在，中国的零售商只在网店卖东西。	□	□
理由：________________________________		
（4）现在，旅游和餐饮都可以通过网购实现。	□	□
理由：________________________________		
（5）很多社会学家都非常关注中国的网购现象。	□	□
理由：________________________________		

拓展练习

话题活动

观看纪录片《家电网购，中国人创造的世界奇迹》和纪录片《走遍中国》中的“网购的力量”，了解中国网购的发展和现状。

话题讨论

1. 采访你的爸爸妈妈或爷爷奶奶，听一听他们对网上购物和不带现金出门消费的看法。

2. 智能手机的发展越来越成熟，智能手机的功能越来越全面。请你说说你自己国家网上购物、电子移动支付的现状。另外谈谈手机对人类学习和生活的影响，包括正面影响和负面影响。

写作练习

有人认为“科技发展给社会带来的正面影响远远大于负面影响”。请你们就此问题分小组辩论。你是正方代表，请围绕“新科技推动社会发展”的观点，用 500 ~ 700 字写出你方的辩论稿。

文化点

电子支付

电子支付是指通过电子手段完成支付过程的一种支付方式，包括网上银行转账、第三方支付、手机银行等多种形式。它基于互联网技术，将传统的支付方式数字化，实现了快速、便捷、安全地进行交易。

在中国，电子支付的应用范围非常广泛。随着电子商务的迅猛发展，电子支付已经成为线上购物的标配。人们可以通过支付宝、微信支付等电子支付平台方便快捷地完成购物支付。此外，电子支付还广泛应用于餐饮、出行、医疗等领域，人们可以通过手机或其他智能设备进行支付，无需携带现金或银行卡。电子支付的普及不仅方便了人们的日常生活，也推动了无纸币社会的进程，大大提高了金融服务的效率，推动了中国的数字化经济发展。

参考答案

话题一　饮食

课文 1　一百元挑战成都小吃街

1.（1）熊猫（1 分）和美食（1 分）
（2）成都建设路
（3）用一百元（人民币）挑战成都小吃街
（4）喜欢吃美食的人

2.（1）C　（2）A　（3）F　（4）B　（5）H

3.（1）对。很多当地人和中外游客都会来这里品尝美食小吃。
（2）对。我是吃货，她也是吃货。
（3）对。李夏天的中文很标准，甚至还会说四川话。
（4）错。她很难接受这个味道。
（5）错。烧仙草是中国南方特色饮品。

课文 2　筷子

1.（1）必须具备；必须备有
（2）逆流而上，向江河发源处走，比喻探索事物的由来
（3）不会烫手的同时也更加方便
（4）表示十分接近；差不多
（5）犯忌讳的话或行动

2.（1）箸
（2）很热（1 分），小块（1 分）
（3）通过手指灵活（1 分）的协调动作（1 分）

3.（1）D　（2）G　（3）A　（4）F　（5）B

话题二　衣着

课文 1　奥运赛场上的中国时尚

1.（1）因为马配上一副讲究的马鞍会显得特别骏美

（2）女装纽扣牡丹纹

（3）叶锦添（1 分）他当年曾凭借《卧虎藏龙》获得奥斯卡“最佳艺术指导”奖（1 分）

（4）图案以文物“五星出东方利中国”（1 分）的祥云瑞兽纹样（1 分）为灵感。

（5）形容人的姿态非凡出众

（6）凤凰图案（1 分），表示着她们用绝美的赛场风姿夺得好成绩的决心（1 分）

（7）缠绵灵动

2.（1）E （2）D （3）G （4）A （5）C

课文 2　苗族银饰

1.（1）C （2）D （3）F （4）G （5）H

2.（1）刺绣（1 分）、银饰（1 分）

（2）（全靠）手工

（3）她们头饰上的银片颤动发出的沙沙声（1 分），胸前项圈的叮当撞击声（1 分）

3.（1）B （2）D （3）A （4）E （5）C

话题三　休闲

课文 1　冰嬉

1.A　B　D　E　F　H

2.（1）娱乐，提高作战灵活性，提高抗寒能力（写出任意两个即可）

（2）清朝宫廷冰上表演的盛况

（3）冰嬉表演队员身着八旗士兵的服饰、脚踏冰鞋进行演出。

3.（1）C　（2）F　（3）A　（4）B　（5）D

课文 2 太极拳

1.（1）C　（2）A　（3）D　（4）C　（5）A

2.（1）错。2020 年“太极拳”被列入联合国教科文组织非物质文化遗产名录。

（2）对。太极拳还融入了中国传统儒家价值观念。

（3）对。从而达到治病健身的效果

（4）错。适合不同年龄的人群

（5）对。太极拳学习者有 4 亿多人。

3.（1）传承　（2）理念　（3）平衡　（4）青睐　（5）传播

话题四　出行

课文 1　中国高铁上的外卖

1.（1）使用手机 APP 点外卖
（2）从上海到广州
（3）鸭肉、茄子、蒸蛋（任选两个）
（4）帕尼尼套餐

2.（1）2017 年 7 月 17 日
（2）94.7%
（3）4 万公里
（4）长三角、珠三角、环渤海等经济发达的地区
（5）四川盆地、云贵高原以及甘肃、新疆等西部地区

3.（1）A （2）B （3）A （4）A （5）A

课文 2　中国的共享单车

1.（1）F （2）A （3）D （4）B （5）H

2.（1）象征着过上了小康生活
（2）智能手机
（3）规定区域内
（4）打开手机上的应用软件（1 分）
因为单车上都装有全球定位系统追踪器（1 分）

3.（1）对。五天的雾霾笼罩，再次唤起了人们对绿色出行的关注。
（2）错。进入 21 世纪，自行车逐渐被汽车取代。
（3）错。以目前规模最大的“哈啰单车”和“美团单车”为例
（4）错。中国的共享单车数量就已经超过了其他国家的总和。
（5）对。令人们的短距离出行变得更加方便

话题五　节庆

课文 1　月饼——中国人亲情的纽带

1.（1）月亮

（2）中国古代四大美女之一

（3）留下一角月饼

（4）表达了人们在中秋节里对团圆的渴望

（5）苏式、京式、广式

2.（1）D　（2）B　（3）A　（4）B　（5）C

3.（1）对。农历八月十五当天，月亮会形成又圆又亮的满月。

（2）对。就口味而言，有甜的也有咸的。

（3）错。月饼除了有代表团圆的传统圆形之外，还有正方、八角、三角等形状。

（4）错。月饼正走向海外市场，成为受人们欢迎的节日食品。

（5）错。但其内涵始终不变

课文 2　泼水节

1.（1）E　（2）D　（3）F　（4）G　（5）C

2.（1）一年一度

（2）祝福

（3）逐渐

（4）能歌善舞

（5）精心制作

3.（1）泼水节是他们寻觅爱情的美好时节。

（2）泼水节可以全面展现傣族的水文化（1 分）、音乐舞蹈文化（1 分）、饮食文化（1 分）、服饰文化（1 分）等传统文化。

话题六　消费

课文 1　祝您用餐愉快

1. （1）手机上下单（1 分），外卖小哥在半小时之内就能将外卖送到（1 分）。
   （2）了解外卖这个行业（1 分），体验中国外卖小哥一天的生活（1 分）。
   （3）不顺利（1 分），因为他不熟悉软件的运用和接单的流程（1 分）。
   （4）因为顾客看都不看他一眼（1 分），也没有说声感谢（1 分），冷漠地接过外卖就关上了大门（1 分）。
   （5）一点儿都不容易 / 需要很强的学习能力 / 需要快速反应的能力（任选一个）
2. （1）B　（2）D　（3）G　（4）A　（5）C

课文 2　“双十一”购物节

1. （1）电商促销日（1 分）和网络购物狂欢日（1 分）
   （2）突破了千亿元人民币
   （3）大山里的新鲜空气
   （4）物流 / 快递（任选一个）
2. （1）C　（2）B　（3）C　（4）A　（5）D
3. （1）对。11 月 11 日是中国最火爆的电商促销日和网络购物狂欢日
   （2）错。除了买衣物和生活用品之外，还可以购买水果蔬菜。
   （3）错。线上线下的充分融合
   （4）对。……餐饮、文化、旅游、教育、金融等产品
   （5）错。很多经济学家认为……

出 品 人：王君校
策划编辑：张　超
责任编辑：杨　晗
英文编辑：范逊敏
封面设计：北京几何创想艺术设计有限公司
排　　版：马　丽
印刷监制：汪　洋

图书在版编目（CIP）数据

中国文化精读教程 . 社会生活 / 冯薇薇，张超编著 . —北京：华语教学出版社，2025.4

ISBN 978-7-5138-2563-4

Ⅰ . ①中… Ⅱ . ①冯… ②张… Ⅲ . ①汉语—对外汉语教学—教材 Ⅳ . ① H195.4

中国国家版本馆 CIP 数据核字 (2024) 第 032854 号

中国文化精读教程・社会生活

冯薇薇 张超 编著

*

华语教学出版社有限责任公司出版
（中国北京百万庄大街 24 号 邮政编码 100037）
电话：(86)10-68320585 68997826
传真：(86)10-68997826 68326333
网址：www.sinolingua.com.cn
电子信箱：hyjx@sinolingua.com.cn
北京虎彩文化传播有限公司印刷
2025 年（16 开）第 1 版
2025 年第 1 版第 1 次印刷
ISBN 978-7-5138-2563-4
007900